To my parents, who supported every one of my creative ventures.

To my grandmother, who opened so many doors through prayer.

To my brothers, who showed me how to lead with love.

To Lisa, who gave me a chance.

To Ash, Viv, Myra, and April, who believed in me when no one else did.

To my husband, who made it possible for all my dreams to come true.

To my high school counselor, who said I wasn't college material.

Thank you.

None of this would be possible without you all.

THE *REAL* REAL ESTATE AGENT

Generate More Leads, Clients, and Referrals by Being Yourself, Having More Fun, and Making a Difference

AARIN CHUNG

THE REAL REAL ESTATE AGENT
Generate More Leads, Sales, and Referrals by Being Yourself, Having More Fun, and Making a Difference

ISBN PAPERBACK: 978-1-5445-3633-0
EBOOK: 978-1-5445-3634-7

CONTENTS

INTRODUCTION

I had never been kicked out of anywhere in my entire life.

I was a straight A student in school and a classic rule follower. I was (and still am) terrified of being in trouble.

Yet, there I was, being forcibly removed and on the verge of tears.

I was out knocking on doors to generate real estate leads, following the advice of a top-producing agent. But just three doors in, someone called the authorities, who promptly (and harshly) ushered me out.

This would have been terrifying for any person. But as a Black person, it was also traumatizing. It's literally the exact scenario your mother warns you about when you're little, and the exact thing you try to avoid for the rest of your life.

And yet, here I was.

The irony of it all? I actually lived in the community that I was getting kicked out of.

So after the dust settled and my tears dried, I walked across the street slowly, let myself back into the community, and walked sullenly all the way home.

Needless to say, I hated door knocking from that day on. So I spent the next year learning how to master lead generation in other ways—both online and in person.

During that time, I also joined a real estate team. And one day the team leader forced us to door knock around one of her new listings to promote its open house. Instantly, I was flooded with a river of raw emotions, but being a team player, I reluctantly agreed to go.

Hoping for the best but preparing for the worst, I decided to run a few ads and schedule a couple social media posts online. If history decided to repeat itself, at least my lead generation time wouldn't be a total loss.

When we arrived at the listing, my team leader handed me 150 flyers and told me to knock on 150 doors. I carefully walked and knocked for the next three hours until I delivered the last flyer.

As I walked back to look for the rest of my team members, I began thinking about how many conversations I'd had. At that moment, I realized that only one person had even bothered to answer the door (then quickly shut it on me when I was in midsentence).

When my team and I reconvened, they all reported similar results. That day, we hand-delivered almost five hundred flyers and had *zero* conversations—what a bust.

Defeated and dismayed, we decided to grab lunch. Someone suggested an amazing new hamburger joint that opened up at the mall, and we all agreed it would be a nice reprieve after so many hours of door knocking.

But as we pulled up to the mall, we saw a long line wrapped around the corner from the entrance. "Is this line for the restaurant?" my team member asked. And unfortunately, it was. This was my second defeat of the day.

Still starving, we got out of the car anyway to find food elsewhere. As we passed the hamburger joint, out of sheer curiosity, my team leader asked the manager why the line was so long. He said they were having a promotional event, and only influencers and bloggers were invited, so everyone else had to stand in line and wait.

As I was about to walk away, my team leader pointed at me and said, "Aarin's an influencer and a blogger. Can we get in?"

I didn't even register what was happening when someone pushed me to a seat, sat me down, and shoved a menu in my face. "Everything on the menu is free, so order whatever you want. Just give us an honest review and write-up online. Cool?" I quickly agreed, thanked the server, and had one of the best meals I've *ever* eaten.

Before leaving the restaurant, I took several photos, wrote up a quick summary of my experience, and posted about it on my blog and social media accounts. I wanted to show the manager that I was grateful for the experience and followed through on my promise, so I walked back to say thank you and showed him my published blog post. I also told him I was an agent and asked him if I could hold one of my events at his bar in the future. He gave me his card and told me to reach out to him about the event but also about real estate—he was thinking about making a move.

As I was driving home, happy to get a free meal and a great lead, I noticed that my phone was buzzing like crazy. I quickly checked my analytics to find that I had tons of new notifications. My blog post went viral and was already shared over two thousand times! The new restaurant was popular, and apparently, I was the first to review it.

People in my community were reaching out to me on social media, opting in to my email list, and following all of my accounts to get notified about future local events.

Then, when I got home, I opened my laptop to find six warm leads from the online ads that I ran earlier that morning. I had totally forgotten.

I then tallied all the leads I received that day:

- Door-Knocking Leads: 0
- In-Person Leads: 1
- Online Ads: 6
- Social Media: 2
- Website: 1
- **Total Leads: 10**

And then it hit me...

We now live in a world where people can move seamlessly between being online and being in person. And that's precisely what I had done that day.

I've come to realize that our reality is now virtual. And virtual is now our reality.

> Our reality became virtual. And virtual became my reality.

Two worlds have collided, and the impact can be felt far and wide.

For the first time in history...

...When you meet buyers at a showing, they've already seen the home online.

...You don't need "listings to last" because now everyone enters the market online as a buyer—even if they have a home to sell.

...You are no longer the gatekeeper of every home because everyone has access to your MLS in their pocket.

...You can't hide a bad client experience because everyone has a voice on the internet.

...Your past clients have incredible influence over future clients when they leave an online review.

...You don't need to generate leads one by one because the internet allows you to do so at scale.

...You can be inundated with leads when you're not even working because the internet allows people to reach you anywhere, anytime, anyplace.

And for the first time in history, you have a critical need to keep up, but your broker, mentor, and coach can't teach you how.

No wonder traditional lead generation methods no longer work. Real estate marketing is broken because the real estate industry has shifted. And most of us missed it.

Old-school agents are lost online because they started before the internet existed. New-school agents are lost in person because they've overautomated relationships. Luddites are paralyzed by the past and technophiles are paralyzed by their programs.

We need to get back to center and refocus on what's important—our clients.

But how?

If you're reading this book, there's a good chance you've been asking this question too.

Maybe you're wondering how to market your business in person when real estate begins exclusively online—or how you're supposed to market online if real estate is experienced exclusively in person.

Or maybe you've even realized that online and in person are now one and the same, which means that you've also recognized the need for an integrated marketing model that unifies them both.

Does any of this sound familiar?

Does this describe you?

If so, ***this is the perfect book for you.***

It was written specifically for agents just like you...

> *...An agent who wants to market for the year we actually live in.*
>
> *...An agent who wants to get more leads, sales, and referrals to grow their real estate business.*
>
> *...An agent who wants to do all of the above by simply being themselves, having more fun, and making a difference.*

I've helped hundreds of thousands of agents all over the globe who all started out just like you.

Maybe you're a new agent who's set to leave your day job—but you need a marketing model that will help you generate enough leads, sales, and referrals to replace your former income.

Maybe you're a seasoned agent who's tried all the "recommended" programs, memberships, courses, games, and gimmicks—and you just want a simple, step-by-step system to help you grow your business.

Or maybe you're a team leader who feels discouraged because the marketing methods you used to grow your business are no longer working—and you need a new way to help you keep the market share you've worked so hard to acquire.

No matter where you are on your journey...

If you want to launch, grow, or scale your real estate business, this book will get you there.

But if this doesn't describe you, then this book probably isn't right for you, and you can put it down and move on to another book that's better suited. (And if you've already paid for it, then just email me directly and I'll give you your money back: aarin@communityinfluencer.com. I'm totally serious.)

But let's say that this does sound like you, and you're in the right place...

By the end of this book, you'll have a modern marketing model that will allow you to attract an infinite number of leads, clients, and referrals so you can scale your business to 7-figures and beyond.

You'll be able to attract more leads, clients, and referrals than you can handle.

You won't have to rely on anyone or anything to grow your real estate business—because it will be self-sustaining.

You'll have a complete marketing strategy—a business in a box—instead of fragmented, one-off tactics.

You'll be able to get in front of more people with less effort, making your business infinitely scalable.

You'll spend less time by marketing on proven platforms that generate proven results.

You'll spend less money by advertising directly to your community instead of indirectly through lead generation vendors.

You'll have omnipresence online (and off)—and appear everywhere, to everyone, all the time.

You'll learn modern marketing methods and fortify your business for the future, so you never get left behind.

You'll market authentically, so you can confidently create a brand presence you love, let your personality shine, and stand out from the crowd.

You'll be able to educate your leads, demonstrate your expertise, and convert leads to clients—before you even meet them.

You'll be seen as the digital mayor of your town, become the go-to agent in your community, and begin to take over your local market.

You'll have all the knowledge you need to grow your real estate business to 7-figures and beyond.

These methods work, as long as you do.

That's my promise to you.

WHAT THIS BOOK WILL TEACH YOU

In this book, I'll teach you a million-dollar marketing model, and here are the exact steps you'll take on your path to success:

STEP 1: THE 7-FIGURE FLYWHEEL® FRAMEWORK

My signature, multimillion-dollar real estate marketing plan.

STEP 2: BUILD A MAGNETIC BRAND

Learn all the real estate branding basics so you can start attracting leads like a magnet.

STEP 3: ATTRACT LEADS TO YOUR LIST

Learn fifty-plus untapped lead sources that will allow you to get new real estate leads, starting today.

STEP 4: CONVERT LEADS INTO CLIENTS

Learn how to nurture warm leads until they're ready to hire you.

STEP 5: TRANSFORM CLIENTS INTO FANS

Learn how to design an unforgettable client experience so clients become raving fans of your brand.

STEP 6: TURN FANS INTO REFERRALS

Learn to build a referral marketing engine that amplifies your reach and increases your revenue.

STEP 7: GAIN INFINITE MOMENTUM

Accelerate your marketing machine so you can grow your business to 7-figures and beyond.

WHAT THIS BOOK WILL *NOT* TEACH YOU

There are a lot of books about real estate marketing, and to be honest, most of them just aren't any good. They're either written by real estate agents who've never been formally trained in marketing, or they're written by marketers who've never been formally trained in real estate.

Let me be clear about what this book will not teach you, so you don't confuse us with them:

- You aren't going to learn any marketing hacks, quick tricks, or silver bullets. If you want your business to thrive long-term, you need to deploy long-term solutions.
- You're not going to learn how to manifest your way to success. Contrary to popular belief, you can't "think and grow rich." Wealth requires work (not woo). So, I'm not going to give you any crystal grids or meditation music. Instead, I'll give you actionable plans that work (as long as you do).
- You're also not going to learn how to buy leads. You're an entrepreneur, not an employee—so you can't rely on anyone or anything to ensure the success of your business, which is why I'm going to teach you how to generate your own leads.
- You're not going to learn operations, because you need to learn marketing first. Marketing is the most significant determining factor of your success in this business. You can be the best real estate agent in the world, but if no one knows, you have no business—just a really expensive hobby. In order to become a millionaire you need to first become a marketer. There's zero correlation between being a great REALTOR® and making money, but there's a direct correlation between being a great marketer and making money. Nothing is more important than generating leads for your business. Nothing. And that's why you need to master marketing before all else.

- You're not going to learn how to outsource the work. If you can't do it, you can't delegate it. And if you try, people will capitalize on your ignorance. You won't know how to hire someone who can do it right (or when to fire someone who's doing it wrong). I don't want anyone to take advantage of you. You've come too far and worked too hard. Do it, then delegate it.
- You won't learn how to lie, cheat, or sleaze your way to success. We teach agents to lead with trust, not transactions, and compassion, not commission. Here's why: As a real estate agent, you'll be helping families live their dreams. As a business owner, you'll hire people and impact their lives. And as a community leader, you'll impact your city, neighborhood, or town. So your job is to serve people, and your marketing needs to align. Relationships first, real estate second.

You probably weren't expecting any of that from this book anyway, but I still needed to say it, to eliminate any doubt.

WHY LISTEN TO ME?

Because I know how to get leads, sales, and referrals for real estate agents.

My name is Aarin Chung. I founded Community Influencer®, the world's largest online learning community for real estate professionals. And I'm the author of this book.

Over the years, I've helped hundreds of thousands of agents grow their real estate businesses via my academy, podcast, show, and various media outlets.

I've worked as a private consultant for top producers, brokerages, and famous celebrity agents.

I have a popular blog that receives tens of thousands of visitors every month, well-known social media channels where I update agents on the latest trends, a viral YouTube channel where I teach lead generation to the masses, and a massive online group where I connect with my community daily.

I've also generated countless leads for countless real estate businesses—including my own.

Every marketing strategy you'll read in this book has been tested and proven by agents all over the country and all over the globe.

I'm not saying any of this to brag, just to make a simple point: you're in good hands.

If any of this resonates with you, then this book is for you.

Let's get started.

STEP 1

THE FLYWHEEL FRAMEWORK

Every marketing strategy that you've ever been taught has been based on a traditional sales funnel.

You've seen this model, right?

At the top of the funnel, they become aware of you.

In the middle, they take interest.

At the bottom, they engage.

And they exit when they eventually buy.

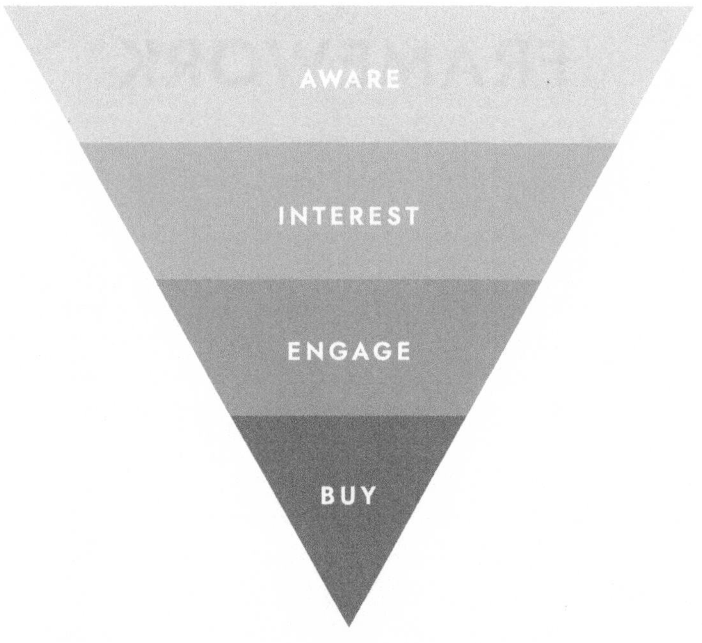

The sales funnel was the first formal marketing theory ever invented. And it's dominated marketing for over a century. It predates the invention of TV, direct mail, telemarketing, the internet, websites, social media, and smartphones—which is why it no longer works.

First, it forces your leads down a linear path. So the lead has to start at the top of the funnel and patiently work their way down. Until recently, this worked flawlessly because every real estate lead started a transaction by meeting with an agent first. But remember, the agent is no longer the gatekeeper of the MLS, so leads now come to the agent last, closer to the bottom. But the sales funnel doesn't allow people to enter through the sides—only the top. So if a lead engages with you on the internet and wants to immediately buy, you have to send them up through the top of the funnel first and wait for them to slowly trickle down. This means that a sales funnel doesn't allow you to get clients unless they were first converted from leads.

Second, a sales funnel also forces your business to become more narrow at the bottom. This worked well until recently because agents typically generated new leads one by one through methods like cold-calling and door knocking. But now, the internet allows agents to generate thousands of leads simultaneously at scale. So if you have lots of leads entering the top who all want to become clients at the bottom, your funnel gets clogged. This means that a sales funnel doesn't allow you to widen your client base because you're constrained by the funnel itself.

Third, a sales funnel also assumes that people at the bottom have no influence over the people at the top. This was primarily true until we got online reviews—which give clients the power to publicly share their experiences with your brand. So now, clients who exit the bottom of your funnel can sell (or repel) new leads who enter at the top. Happy clients amplify opportunities for referrals. Unhappy clients echo opportunities for improvement. But the sales funnel doesn't account for either because there's no connection between the bottom and the top. This is a massive problem in a new world that's hyperfocused on customer experience.

So we need to get back to basics.

We have to come back to center and refocus on what's important—the client. Because the client never changes.

Technology comes and goes, but the client never will.

So we need to put them at the center of our businesses. And that's precisely why we abandoned the funnel and adopted the flywheel.

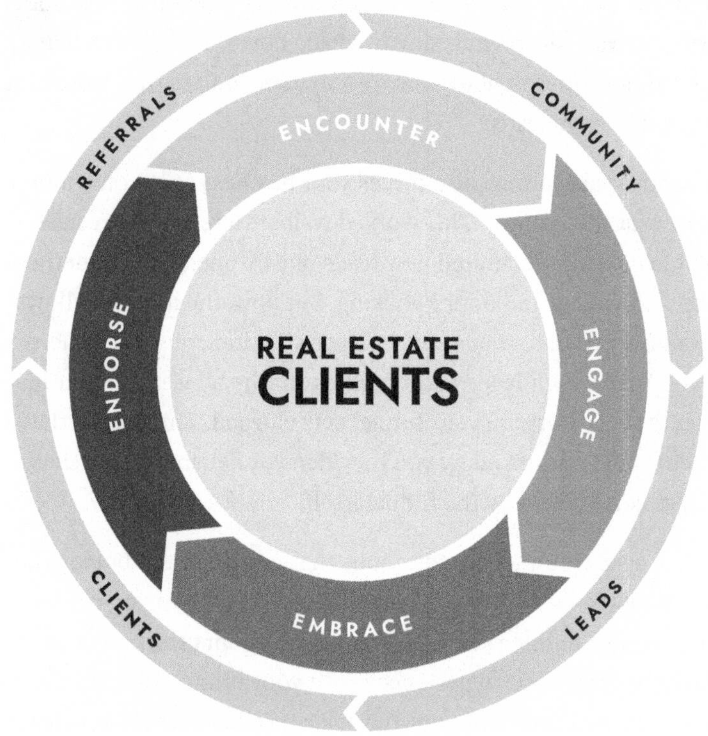

A flywheel is a heavy disc that requires initial force to spin. And once it starts spinning, it will never stop—unless you apply friction. Flywheels are so effective that they've been used for centuries in pottery wheels, sewing machines, factory equipment, transportation, rechargeable batteries, and now, your real estate business.

I created the 7-Figure Flywheel® to be a self-sustaining marketing model that makes momentum through a steady stream of leads, clients, and referrals.

In the outer ring, there are four sections:

First, community members become leads, then leads become clients, then clients become referrals, and finally, referrals become members of your community. It's an infinite, scalable cycle.

In the inner ring, there are four stages:

1. **Encounter:** When your community becomes aware of your brand
2. **Engage:** When your brand communicates with its leads
3. **Embrace:** When your brand is loved by its clients
4. **Endorse:** When your brand is recommended via referrals

Then referrals encounter your brand. And the whole cycle begins again.

At the center of your flywheel, everything revolves around the client. And unlike a funnel, people can enter the flywheel at different places, times, or marketing channels. But the end result will always be the same—a new client.

Clients are no longer taking a linear path.

Because marketing is no longer a straight line.

It's now a circle.

And everything in that circle revolves around the client.

The beauty of the flywheel is that it's a plug-and-play model. This means that you can plug in any marketing strategy you want at any stage of your flywheel in order to gain momentum.

In upcoming chapters, I'm going to give you every real estate marketing tactic under the sun. But don't get overwhelmed. You don't need to implement every tactic at once—in fact, I recommend that you don't.

If you're a new agent, you can plug in just one strategy until you master it, then add more when you're ready. If you're a seasoned agent, you can plug in as many strategies as you can handle solo. And if you're a team leader, you can plug in as many strategies as your team can handle together.

That's what makes the flywheel so special. It can grow with your business initially and expand to the extent that you do!

I want you to think of this entire book as a reference—something you work through, work on, then keep coming back to. Why? Because in the great words of Albert Einstein, you should "never memorize something that you can look up."

Learn. Plug. Play. Come back another day.

There's no pressure to do it all. Just learn and implement the strategies that feel most comfortable to you at your own pace. If you love YouTube, start there. If you love open houses, start with that. If you prefer websites, the world is yours.

It's your business, and it's your choice. And I'll give you tons of choices to choose from.

But there's one caveat: avoid friction at all costs.

Isaac Newton's first law of motion states that an object in motion stays in motion—unless friction is applied.

Friction includes anything that constrains your business from getting results. I'll give you lots of examples throughout this book, but a few of the most obvious examples are things like poor customer experience, processes, communication, marketing, branding, messaging, and follow-up.

If you can stay hyperfocused on applying force, while also being careful to avoid friction, your flywheel will spin infinitely.

This means you can finally go on vacation or take an extended break without losing any momentum.

It also means that you can scale your business exponentially.

And in the following chapters, I'll show you how.

STEP 2

BUILD A MAGNETIC BRAND

2.1

MARKET TO SELL

Before we dive deeper into the flywheel framework, we need to get on the same page about what marketing is (and isn't). So, let's define the term: **marketing**.

The textbook definition is long and confusing, so let me make it simple...

Know what people want, then help them get it. *That's it.*

That's how marketing makes you money. It's such a simple sentence, but there is a lot to unpack. And the best way to do that is through the seven Cs.

THE SEVEN CS OF MARKETING

1. **Clients:** People who want your services and are willing and able to pay for them
2. **Creativity:** The injection of your imagination, style, and personality
3. **Consistency:** Something done on a regular, reliable cadence for a very long time
4. **Communication:** When people listen and feel compelled to take action
5. **Convenience:** The elimination of friction
6. **Credibility:** When people believe you because you're trustworthy
7. **Competition:** Other people who can offer the same services to your clients

1. CLIENTS

Clients are people who want your services and are willing and able to pay for them. However, there's an old adage that says, "When your target market is everyone, you are special to no one." So contrary to popular belief, "everyone" should never be your target market. Instead, your target market should only include people whom you are willing and able to work with. Let's start with the latter.

People you're typically *unable* to work with:

- Minors
- Other real estate agents
- Out-of-towners (with no intent to move into your market)

People you may be *unwilling* to work with:

- People who are too far away from your service area
- People who are untrustworthy, unscrupulous, or unethical

You may not align with these characteristics, so these people may not be a good fit for your business. But everyone else is fair game!

Once you're speaking to the right people, the next step is to create memorable marketing that resonates by making your messaging relevant. The best way to ensure that your message is relevant is to think of one ideal client you'd love to work with, then design your marketing to attract more people like that one person. In marketing, this is called an "avatar." An avatar allows you to create focused, relevant messaging that resonates with your target market. At Community Influencer®, our avatar is named Adrian.

MEET ADRIAN

Adrian is a creative, modern, hardworking agent who wants to get more leads, clients, and referrals to help more families find homes. Adrian also loves learning new things, meeting new people, and finding new ways to grow her business. Adrian is caring, is kind, and knows how to have a good time!

Adrian probably sounds a lot like you—and that's by design. When we market, we carefully choose every word, graphic, and image with Adrian in mind. I speak directly to Adrian in all of our marketing, which is why we now have hundreds of thousands of "Adrians" in our community. You being here is not an accident. It's a direct result of careful planning and processes. In this book, I'll teach you how to attract thousands of ideal clients to your business too!

But first, let's look at four possible avatars from around the country.

AVATAR #1:
KURT IN BOULDER, CO

Kurt is an avid outdoorsman who enjoys hiking in the summer, skiing in the winter, and good local microbrews all year round.

AVATAR #2:
ELISE IN NEW YORK, NY

Elise is a VIP socialite with access to the most exclusive clubs, restaurants, and shows in the city.

AVATAR #3:
EVELYN IN RANCHO PALOS VERDES, CA

Evelyn is an equestrian who loves horseback riding, show jumping, eventing, and dressage.

AVATAR #4:
WALTER IN NAPLES, FL

Walter is a retiree who is big into boating, golfing, and dining at five-star restaurants.

Customer avatars give you a general idea of your ideal client, but we also need to know their motivations. Understanding *why* they may be looking to buy or sell a home is what makes your marketing resonate. The easiest way to get to your avatar's "why" is to ask yourself, "What would they consider a job well done?" Asking this question will allow you to understand their motivation and enable you to market in a way that matters.

Let's take another look at our four avatars through the lens of a "job well done." First, there's Kurt, our outdoorsman who loves microbrews. What would Kurt consider a job well done? From talking with other clients like Kurt, you might already know that Kurt started in the suburbs of Boulder, when money was tight. His current home is fine, but he's longing for that "cabin in the woods" vibe. He's saved up enough money and wants to finally love where he lives.

It can be tempting to just toss up an ad that says, "Stunning home with quick access to all Boulder has to offer!" But that's not going to get Kurt's attention. So instead, think about why someone with Kurt's particular passions would be looking at real estate listings in the first place. There's a good chance that his current home isn't in a place where he can do all the things he loves without a long commute.

So a job well done for Kurt would be living closer to where he vacations. And with just that little extra bit of information, our ad is transformed into...

AD #1:
KURT IN BOULDER, CO

Live where you vacation with this stunning cabin, close to everything Golden Canyon State Park has to offer!

Now that's an ad that would get Kurt's attention!

Next up, Elise, the VIP socialite who spends her time out and about in NYC, partying it up in the city's most exclusive clubs, dining in the city's best restaurants, and taking in the city's hottest shows.

Elise has worked incredibly hard since coming to New York, and she finally has the money and freedom to enjoy the lifestyle she wants. She's looking for a home that is in a trendy area with easy access to the excitement, fun, and finer things the city has to offer. Are you going to win her over with homes in Weehawken, New Jersey? Not a chance. Just mentioning the Lincoln Tunnel is enough to make her eyes glaze over. If it isn't the trendiest area of Manhattan, she is not interested because it's not what she would consider a job well done.

To attract clients like Elise, your marketing needs headlines that emphasize the trendiness of the area and everything within her reach. For example, to get Elise's attention on a social media post, you could write something like...

AD #2:
ELISE IN NEW YORK, NY

White-glove service and top-of-the-line amenities in the heart of East Village.

Next up, Evelyn, the equestrian. What drives Evelyn? Perhaps she has a couple of horses but has been paying for stable space because she doesn't have a barn on her property. She's looking for a new home and a new property where she can bring her horses back under her care and maybe even add a few more into the mix.

What would Evelyn consider a job well done? Your listings need headlines emphasizing the property and its potential as a home for horses. If you wanted to grab her attention using an email subject line, it would read...

AD #3:
EVELYN IN RANCHO PALOS VERDES, CA

Your dream home: a sprawling, Rolling Hills equestrian estate.

And finally, we have Walter. Walter is retired and living his best life boating, golfing, and eating the most delicious food. So how can you attract clients like Walter? You already know that Walter likes to stay active, but you've also discovered two things that can help attract him and clients like him. First, he's looking for an upscale home that's a bit smaller than his current home, now that his children are grown. Second, he hates stairs.

What would Walter consider a job well done? Walter's looking for a "right-sized" home that he can navigate for the rest of his life, regardless of what happens to his health—no stairs allowed! So marketing to Walter would read...

AD #4:
WALTER IN NAPLES, FL

Live closer to the things you love! This beautiful single-story has all the space and none of the stairs.

If you don't already know what your local audience wants, there's a simple solution. It may sound silly, but sitting down for a drink or coffee with your ideal client is a great way to get to know them better. By taking the time to do this, you'll be armed with the knowledge to create magnetic marketing that attracts your local avatar.

Now that we've covered what an avatar is and what they would consider a job well done, you've nailed your niche! But how do you know if you got it right?

The easiest way to know when you've nailed your niche is to use a test called the "Party Pitch." If I left a party early and, in my absence, someone asked, "Hey, what does Aarin do?," would people at the party be able to explain it accurately?

If they said, "Oh, Aarin? She teaches real estate agents how to make more money by getting more clients," then I've nailed my niche. But if they said, "Aarin does marketing for real estate agents" or "Oh, I'm not really sure," then I haven't nailed my niche. Your brand is the essence of what people say about you after you've left the room. If people can't pitch your business on your behalf, it also means they can't refer your business either—and that's a big problem.

To overcome this obstacle, ask people what they think you do, then see if they can accurately describe who you help and why. Do this until you pass the "Party Pitch" test, then you'll know you've nailed your niche!

Now that you know whom you serve, it's time to talk about what they want. The number one rule of marketing is "What's in it for me?" (WIIFM). People only care about your marketing when they know how it can specifically benefit them. Therefore, all of your marketing has to clearly and effectively communicate what's in it for your ideal client. If your message is all about you, no one will listen.

I can't tell you how many bus-stop benches I've seen with an ad featuring an agent, folding their arms, and the words, "Call me."

What? Why? You haven't even given me a reason to call, let alone to trust you as a reliable agent. This is the lowest form of marketing there is, because it's designed for the agent, not the audience.

In every marketing campaign you run, always ask yourself...

What's in it for them?

What do they want?

HINT:

Buyers want homes.

Sellers want money.

Residents want community.

Let's go back to our four avatars one more time. Kurt in Colorado wants to sell his starter home in the suburbs to buy a quiet cabin in the mountains. Elise wants a list of fun events happening tomorrow night to meet new people. Evelyn wants a list of horse properties with direct access to trails. And Walter wants a list of one-story homes, so he can make the most of his retirement in Florida.

No one cares to know how many homes you've sold, how many awards you've received, or how much market share your broker has obtained. If you want people to pay attention to you, pay attention to the people.

2. CREATIVITY

Creativity is our second Marketing C. Creativity is the injection of your unique imagination, style, and personality. Scott Stratten once said, "If you're your authentic self, you have no competition." And this couldn't be more true when it comes to marketing. But it seems like every agent wants to look exactly like their competition.

This is the worst marketing strategy a business can have. From a lead's point of view, you all look alike, talk alike, act alike, and sound alike. So how on earth are they supposed to pick you out of a crowd? Short answer: they can't.

Be different! Be *yourself*!

We'll talk more about this in the branding chapter, but for now, just know that the colors, designs, fonts, and photos you use matter because they dictate how your brand is perceived. Creativity sells, and I'll show you how in the next chapter.

3. CONSISTENCY

Consistency is our third Marketing C. Consistency is something done on a regular, reliable cadence for a very long time. Whenever I see agents give up on their current marketing strategy to chase another shiny object, I die a little inside.

Stop listening to other agents who get quick results from the latest marketing fads. They're usually not telling you that they have fifty-seven other long-term tactics they've been running in the background for months. It's usually that fifty-eighth thing that gives them a quick little boost, so that's the thing that gets all the credit. That's not how marketing works.

Marketing is a halo. Every time you plug in a new tactic, it compounds on the last. Essentially, the more tactics you stack, the more compounding occurs, and the wider your halo becomes. This is why even the most sophisticated marketers can't attribute all of their results to just one marketing tactic—because it's a combination of multiple marketing tactics.

When you're marketing, never mistake causation for correlation. Causation attributes optimization to one variable. Correlation attributes optimization across many variables. Let's take that a step further.

If you're marketing on both YouTube and Facebook (also known as Meta) and you got three new leads, it's impossible to say for certain that YouTube was 100 percent the cause because YouTube and Facebook have become correlated. When you run both marketing campaigns simultaneously, they each compound on the results of the other.

When the client contacts you, they may tell you that they found you on YouTube, because that's the last marketing channel they remember seeing you on. But they may not have even realized that they saw every single one of your Facebook posts the year before. In this case, that one YouTube video may have *caused* the call, but the call was also correlated to all of the work you put in last year. That's why consistency is critical, especially in a flywheel marketing model. The more momentum you gain, the wider your halo becomes.

An old adage in marketing, "The Rule of Seven," says that a person must hear a brand's message at least seven times before they'll take action or buy. But this rule was created in the 1930s—well before the internet. Now, the average person sees between four thousand and ten thousand ads a day. So, it probably takes seven times before they even *notice* your brand (and seventy-seven before they take action). Suppose you're marketing to someone once a week. That equates to almost two months before they even notice you. And up to eighteen months before they ever take action.

You could have used Facebook to get in front of them seventy-six times, but on the seventy-seventh time, you happened to try a shiny new YouTube video, and that's when they happened to reach out. Again, it's not that your Facebook posts didn't work, it's that your marketing stack compounded, which created a halo that finally pushed them to call.

Now, just imagine how much quicker a lead would notice your brand if you compounded three marketing tactics into your stack instead of two! When I was a new agent, I chose to master blogging, open houses, and Facebook ads—in that order.

Blogging allowed me to learn the nuances of my local neighborhood, which then gave me the confidence to do open houses. And Facebook ads allowed me to promote my open houses, which gave me tons of traffic and leads. The halo around my flywheel was so strong that people would walk into my open houses and introduce themselves to me! They already knew me, because they had already read my blog or seen one of my ads and felt totally comfortable speaking to me at my open house. This was an amazing position to be in as an agent, because I never had to chase people down—they came to me.

It's also how I was able to generate thousands of new leads as a brand-new agent, in a brand-new market, with no sphere of influence. Consistency was my key. I simply mastered one marketing tactic and worked it consistently, then I mastered additional tactics and worked those consistently as well—one at a time, layer by layer.

Consistency is the most significant competitive advantage you have, because most people give up too soon. If you can do something well, and do it consistently, you'll dominate 100 percent of your competitors 100 percent of the time.

4. COMMUNICATION

Communication, our fourth Marketing C, occurs when people listen to you and take action. But people can only hear you if you're speaking close enough to be heard, right? So being heard requires you to speak close to your people. To do this, simply communicate on the marketing channels where you can be heard.

Depending on your goal, sometimes your message is heard best on popular modern channels and sometimes it's heard best on quieter traditional channels.

TRADITIONAL CHANNELS	MODERN CHANNELS
Print Newspapers	Websites
Television	Video
Radio	Podcasts
Phone Calls	Texts, Messages, Chats
In-Person Networking	Facebook Groups
Snail Mail	Email
Door Knocking	Social Media Postings
Print Ads	Online Ads
Phone Book	Online Directories

Once you tune into the channels where people are actively listening, you need to craft a compelling message that moves people to action. In marketing, every word you say either sells or repels.

> In marketing, every word you say either sells or repels.

Let me give you an example.

In this book, you're going to learn how to:

- Build a Magnetic Brand
- Attract Leads to Your List
- Convert Leads into Clients
- Transform Clients into Fans
- Turn Fans into Referrals
- Gain Infinite Momentum

I specifically chose words like "build," "attract," "convert," "transform," "turn," and "gain" because they're powerful words that compel people to take action. In marketing, the act of using words to sell is called copywriting. In the next chapter, I'll show you how.

5. CONVENIENCE

Convenience is our fifth Marketing C. It happens when you remove any friction that makes it harder for people to hire or pay you.

Friction is like a speed bump on a freeway. And as a business owner, it's your job to remove the speed bumps, in pursuit of an effortless client experience. Now, I know you may be asking yourself, "Who would ever add friction to their business?" My answer: every business owner in the world.

We all do it. I've done it. You've done it. You're probably doing it *right now.*

Don't believe me? Check one of your social media bios. Did you specifically include all (or any) of the cities you serve? If you're posting on Instagram but haven't told people where you even work, you've made it harder for people to hire you and give you money. That, my friend, is friction in action.

As a business owner, you have to be actively conscious of friction and eliminate it daily. If you aren't careful, it will creep in. And you may not even realize the hurdles for people who are trying to hire and/or pay you.

My husband, Howard, and I recently moved from one area of Southern California to another. Unfortunately, the new market was an hour and a half away, which meant that we could only look for homes on the weekends, when we weren't working.

We were desperately searching for a new home, and we were ready to drop a few million to make that dream come true. And yet, every weekend we encountered agents who were unavailable, knew nothing about the market, treated us poorly, refused us entry on the weekends, ignored us, never called us back to schedule showings, or allowed us to tour a dirty house.

Why would any agent do this?

It's because friction crept in, and they didn't even notice.

But for heaven's sake, if people are trying to give you money, let them! Remove paywalls, eliminate friction daily, and keep it convenient.

Another way that agents create inconvenience is through poor communication. Traditionally, other real estate coaches tell you that a lead only "counts" when you have a phone number.

First of all, that's ridiculous, because anyone who wants to work with you is a real person, and every person "counts." Second, who still uses their phone to make calls?! (Unless you're my husband, my parents, or a close friend, I'm not answering. And I'm sure your leads feel the same way!)

Instead, meet your leads where they are. Allow them to interact with you where they want.

Facebook message? Cool.

Instagram DM? Perfect.

Text message? You betcha.

Who cares what platform they contacted you on, as long as they did! Why would you turn away business because the lead asked for help on a YouTube comment instead of your landline?

I don't care if someone sends you a message in a bottle or a note via a raven. Act on it! They're trying to give you money. Don't make it difficult.

I specifically designed the flywheel as a circle so your business could be client-centered. People can enter your flywheel whenever they want, however they want, wherever they want. If you want to create momentum in your business, accelerate your flywheel fast and avoid friction at all costs.

6. CREDIBILITY

Credibility is our sixth Marketing C. Being credible means that people believe you because you're trustworthy. So credibility is powered by trust. But trust can only occur when you say what you mean and mean what you say.

If you say you're going to do something, do it.

If you say you're not going to do something, don't do it.

When you break trust, you lose your credibility and, ultimately, your reputation. Warren Buffett once said, "It takes twenty years to build a reputation and five minutes to ruin it. If you think about that, you'll do things differently." He's right.

These days, your reputation is always on the line. Remember, unhappy clients now have a voice to broadcast their concerns. To keep your credibility intact, always stay true to your word, and operate in integrity. Your reputation (and your business) depend on it.

7. COMPETITION

Competition is our final Marketing C. Competition is defined as another person or company that can offer the same services to your clients.

Did that just give you the chills? It should have.

Currently, one out of every ten people has a real estate license in California. The competition here is fierce. And every agent's job is to stand out from them all.

Your marketing should highlight the valuable talents, abilities, education, skills, characteristics, ethics, and creativity that you bring to the table. Again, stop trying to blend in. It creates brand confusion in your marketplace, and a confused customer never buys.

To eliminate competition, you have to learn how to position yourself as the obvious choice. Because the truth is: if you don't define your brand, your competitors will.

FULL CIRCLE

A true marketing strategy has nothing to do with posting on social media, running an ad, filming a video, designing a business card, or printing a fancy flyer. These are all just marketing *tactics*, and marketing tactics change constantly. But a solid marketing strategy never does.

Business owners have been using the same marketing strategy for thousands of years. It's literally called "marketing" because people would set up shop at a marketplace to sell their goods. And two thousand years ago, a shop owner's marketing strategy was the same strategy I'm teaching you today.

If a merchant was selling pomegranates back then, his strategy would be to:

1. Understand the market demand (Customers)

2. Attract people to his booth (Creativity)

3. Show up every day (Consistency)

4. Advise people which fruits to choose (Communication)

5. Provide an effortless customer experience (Convenience)

6. Deal honestly during the sale (Credibility)

7. Ensure his customers come back to his booth (Competition)

That's his whole marketing strategy. A marketing tactic might be yelling loudly throughout the marketplace, holding up a sign, or positioning his booth to increase visibility. But these tactics are just small bits and pieces of a broader strategy. And that strategy is exactly the same today.

Today, your marketing strategy might look something like this:

1. Understand the market demand (Clients)

2. Attract people to your brand (Creativity)

3. Show up every day (Consistency)

4. Advise people about real estate (Communication)

5. Provide an effortless client experience (Convenience)

6. Deal honestly during escrow (Credibility)

7. Ensure your clients come back to you (Competition)

A good marketing tactic might be posting on social media or creating a video, but, just like the merchant yelling about pomegranates in the marketplace, these tactics are just small bits and pieces of a broader marketing strategy.

Any agent with an internet connection can learn to run a Facebook ad, set up a bot campaign, or buy leads from Zillow. But if these trending tactics aren't part of an overarching strategy, composed of compounded layers, they won't work in the long term. I saw this unfold firsthand when the iOS 14 update slayed every agent who put all of their eggs in the Facebook ads basket. Their businesses came to an immediate halt, and became stuck in the Encounter Stage of the flywheel, because they were no longer being seen. This could have been easily prevented if they had only taken the time to master and layer one additional tactic.

I also know agents whose businesses get stuck in the Engage Stage after they put all their eggs in Zillow's basket. They're buying leads for tens of thousands of dollars a month, but they come to me because they don't know how to move these leads to the Embrace Stage, so half of their leads never convert to clients. Can you imagine spending $1.2 million a year on leads only to throw half of them in the trash?

This is why it's so important to have the right marketing strategy and compounded marketing tactics. When agents stop using one-off tactics and start creating a halo with their flywheel, their ROI always increases. But when they don't take the time to strategize, they're always leaving money on the table.

Stop putting all your eggs in one basket. Instead, diversify with a solid strategy. Even the smallest increase in conversion rates can equate to hundreds of thousands of dollars in revenue. Some agents are so close to hitting 7-Figures, but they never will—because they're using shiny tactics instead of enduring strategies.

Do we teach the latest and greatest tactics? Yes. We even have Accelerator Courses in our membership dedicated entirely to the most up-to-date and excellent marketing tactics.

But these tactics are always taught as part of a greater strategy and through the lens of the flywheel framework.

Having a clear strategy is the marketing mindset you need as a business owner. When you make that subtle shift, leads will convert seamlessly from stage to stage, your flywheel will accelerate rapidly, and you'll gain infinite momentum. That's how marketing makes you money!

FORCE VERSUS FRICTION

Apply Force: What levers create momentum in your business?

- Having the right mindset about marketing
- Knowing who your avatar is and what they want
- Showing up consistently
- Injecting your unique style and personality into your marketing
- Communicating on channels where you can be heard
- Eliminating friction
- Being credible and trustworthy
- Standing out from your competition

Avoid Friction: What levers slow momentum in your business?

- Having the wrong mindset about marketing
- Not knowing who your avatar is or what they want
- Showing up sporadically
- Creating confusion in the marketplace by blending in
- Communicating on channels where people aren't listening
- Applying friction
- Losing credibility and trust
- Not standing out from your competition

2.2

BRAND TO SELL

Branding increases your bottom line because it keeps you from becoming a commodity.

A commodity is a product or service that's available everywhere. And because the supply (of that commodity) is so high, the perceived price is low. So, in essence, if you have to choose between two identical products, the cheapest product becomes the most valuable.

In other words, if you can buy a pair of shoes at any booth in the swap meet, shoppers will always buy them from the stall that sells them for less. In this case, the cheapest shoes are the most valuable, because all the shoes have been commoditized. But the second you add a brand name on the shoe, the value goes up. People pay far more for Nike, Jimmy Choo, Louboutin, and Manolo because these brands have a higher perceived value. And as a result, these brands don't have to compete on price.

Your business is no different. If two agents look identical, the lead can't tell the difference and will always choose the cheapest. In this case, the agent who offers to take less commission is most valuable because both agents have become commoditized.

But building a strong brand prevents this from happening. Branding influences the lead's perception of your value, so you're no longer seen as a commodity and can command a higher price. In other words, *you* become Nike, Jimmy Choo, Louboutin, and Manolo.

Better brands are more valuable, so better brands make more money. In this chapter, I'll show you how to build a better brand. First, I'll give you a quick cheat sheet that contains an outline of all the elements needed to build a strong brand. Then, I'll break each element down individually, so you can incorporate each one of them into your business.

BRANDING CHEAT SHEET

Branding Elements:

- **Brand Identity:** Who you think you are
  - **Mission:** Your company's purpose
  - **Vision:** Your company's compass
  - **Values:** What's important to you
  - **Positioning:** Why your customers should choose you
- **Formal Identity:** How you present yourself to the world
  - **Verbal Identity:** Messaging
    - Name
    - Slogan

    - › Copy
  - **Visual Identity:** Design
    - › Logo
    - › Colors
    - › Fonts
- **Brand Image:** Who your clients think you are
  - **Perceptions:** How your brand is perceived
  - **Interactions:** How your brand interacts with clients
  - **Emotions:** How your brand makes people feel
  - **Memories:** How your brand is remembered

BRAND MISSION: YOUR COMPANY'S PURPOSE

Your mission is your brand's reason for existing (exclusive of making money). In essence, it's what you do, whom you serve, and how. Let me give you two examples.

TESLA'S MISSION STATEMENT:

To accelerate the world's transition to sustainable energy.

COMMUNITY INFLUENCER'S MISSION STATEMENT:

To glorify God by helping local business owners increase their income, so they can increase their impact.

A solid mission statement allows you to connect with your clients emotionally—which ultimately drives people to choose your service over another.

CREATE YOUR MISSION STATEMENT

To create a strong brand mission, ask yourself:

- What inspired me to become an agent?
- Why do I continue to be an agent?
- How will being an agent help me achieve my dreams?
- What problems do my clients have?
- How can my brand help my clients solve these problems?
- What emotional needs does my brand address for my clients?
- How does my brand inspire them to achieve their dreams?
- How does my brand help them overcome their fears?
- How do our services allow us to improve our clients' lives?
- How does my brand improve the world?
- How does my brand care for the environment?
- How does my brand improve people's emotional health?

Once you've answered all these questions, look for a general theme that conveys what you do, whom you serve, and how. Once you have that theme, it will become the foundation of your mission statement.

BRAND VISION: YOUR COMPANY'S COMPASS

Your vision is your North Star. It serves as a vital compass and ensures you never get lost.

MICROSOFT'S ORIGINAL VISION STATEMENT:

A computer on every desk and in every home.

COMMUNITY INFLUENCER'S VISION STATEMENT:

To democratize entrepreneurship by becoming the world's largest resource for local business owners.

When Microsoft created their vision, it kept employees focused on designing, producing, and distributing personal computers. Then if someone randomly suggested that they start selling printers, everyone in the company would be able to identify the misalignment.

Likewise, if someone at my company suggested that we start serving large corporations instead of small businesses, anyone on my team would be able to reject the idea by simply pointing back to our company's vision.

Again, when your market is everyone, you're special to no one. So, to keep your brand from being commoditized, you need a strong vision that attracts the best and repels the rest. Your vision should inspire and motivate your clients to action, so that you can stand out from every competitor in your market.

Remember Evelyn, the equestrian? She needs an agent who knows how to help her buy a horse property. And Walter, the retiree—he needs someone who knows Naples, inside and out. Your vision will keep you laser-focused on your clients' needs and keep you from offering services outside of your wheelhouse.

CREATE YOUR VISION STATEMENT

To create a strong brand vision, ask yourself:

- What do I want my brand to look like in the future?
- Where is my business headed?
- What do I want to accomplish as a business?
- Is this vision realistic and attainable?
- Does this vision inspire me?
- Will this vision inspire my clients to take action?
- Is this vision simple and easy to understand?
- Is this vision clear and easy to communicate?

Once you have a good idea of your vision, think of the milestones that occur along the way. These milestones will allow you to accomplish your vision. To ensure that your vision stays client-centric, it should clearly state how your brand will positively impact the lives of your clients.

BRAND VALUES: WHAT'S IMPORTANT TO YOU

Wouldn't it be cool to attract, hire, and lead a team of people you can trust? Getting clear on your values will help you define your company culture. Values define how you act when no one's watching.

GOOGLE'S BRAND VALUES:

Focus on the user, and all else will follow

It's best to do one thing really, really well

Fast is better than slow

Democracy on the web works

You don't need to be at your desk to need an answer

You can make money without doing evil

There's always more information out there

The need for information crosses all borders

You can be serious without a suit

Great just isn't good enough

COMMUNITY INFLUENCER'S BRAND VALUES:

Get closer to the customer

Everything you do sells or repels

Simplicity, never complexity

Identify the opportunity, overcome the obstacle

Audit before you act

Say what needs to be said, even when it's hard

Leverage collective genius, but reject groupthink

There's always an option C

Celebrate every win (and every failure)

Rest is just as important as work

Always do what's best for Community Influencer®

CREATE YOUR BRAND VALUES

To create strong brand values, ask yourself:

- What positive values did I embrace as a child?
- How do I like to be treated when I encounter other brands?
- How do I define a job well done?
- Have I cherished these values since childhood? Or are they merely just a trend?
- What behavior really annoys me?
- Do these values represent my brand's current actions?
- Do these values represent who we are now, instead of who we want to become?
- Are these values represented when no one else is watching?

Take note of any recurring themes, then create up to a few memorable values that accurately represent your brand.

POSITIONING: WHY CLIENTS CHOOSE YOU

The term "positioning" was invented when stores started stocking shelves with products. It literally references the position of your product on the store's shelves. For instance, a cereal brand that caters to kids typically positions its products on store shelves about three feet high—which happens to be within reach of a child. If the store placed the cereal higher on the shelves, the child may never even see it. Similarly, positioning your business in the marketplace allows your ideal customers to reach your brand and services.

WALMART'S BRAND POSITIONING:

Lowest price

COMMUNITY INFLUENCER'S BRAND POSITIONING:

Attainable education

Brand positioning is a critical business decision. It defines why a client should choose you over your competition. Bold positioning mitigates commoditization and allows you to compete in a league of your own.

CREATE YOUR BRAND POSITIONING

To create strong brand positioning, ask yourself:

- Where does my ideal client live?
- How much home can they typically afford?
- Are they married or single?
- Do they have kids?
- What do they like?
- What do they hate?
- What websites do they visit online?
- What social media channels do they use?
- Who is the ideal avatar I'm hoping to attract?
- Who is the avatar I'm hoping to repel?
- What do we do better than anyone else in our market?
- What do we contribute?
- What makes my service unique?
- What are we doing differently to achieve results?
- What would make a lead want to choose me over another?
- If I launched this positioning, would my competitors be jealous?

You'll know when you've nailed your positioning because people will take notice and talk about your brand (because it's different).

FORMAL IDENTITY: HOW YOU PRESENT YOURSELF TO THE WORLD

Creating a formal identity today is crucial because it has the power to lower your marketing costs tomorrow. If people can quickly identify your brand and share it with others, you don't have to pay as much to advertise it. And ultimately, the ability to do both comes down to the messaging and design. Let's start with messaging.

VERBAL IDENTITY: YOUR MESSAGING

A brand's verbal identity consists of its name, slogan, and copy. Let's cover each of these now.

Brand Name: How People Identify Your Brand

Most real estate agents choose their name to represent their brand because it's quick and easy. There's no extra paperwork to file, and agents have been told, for years, that they are their brand. This is why many agents still put their face and name on all their business cards—and real estate is the only industry that does.

Here's why: before the internet, when someone was standing in front of your sign and wanted to see your listing, they needed to be able to remember your name. They didn't have cell phones back then, so they would have to memorize the name, drive home, then look it up in the phone book.

Today, no one needs to remember anything. In a modern world, leads know about your listing before they even drive up to the house. And if they happen to stumble upon a listing while they're out and about, they can just look up the listing on their phone or text you immediately or take a photo to remember it for later. So, technically, agents don't need to use their legal name as their business name anymore.

Did I just hear a sigh of relief from every female agent around the world? I can relate. I spent a small fortune to update all of my paperwork, signage, and marketing after my wedding. From then on, I started looking for other, more permanent ways to name my brand!

Here are just a few...

FOUNDER NAMES:

The traditional naming convention that takes on the name of the person who founded the brand

Ex: Aarin Chung or Keller Williams Realty

Descriptive Names:

Describes a product or service

Ex: Real Estate Maximums, a.k.a. RE/MAX

Metaphoric Names:

Evokes a metaphor that positions the brand

Ex: Compass or Community Influencer®

Made-up Names:

Invented for distinction

Ex: eXp Realty

Acronym Names:

Abbreviated names that contain a few letters and numbers

Ex: C21, a.k.a. Century 21

Geographic Names:

References and reflects a specific geographic location, history, or community

Ex: Your Orange County

For local real estate agents, I prefer geographic names, because a geographic brand name instantly attracts the attention of people looking to buy, sell, or live in that local community.

As an agent, it's sometimes difficult to choose anything other than a founder name because local regulations haven't kept up with modern marketing. But I wanted you to know that you have options—even if you have to file extra paperwork and fork over a small fee.

No matter what name you choose, keep the following best practices in mind:

- Never use the word "REALTOR®" because it's trademarked.
- Only use the word "Realty" or "Real Estate" if you are a brokerage.
- Check all social media platforms to ensure that the brand name isn't already in use.
- Ensure that the domain is still available.
- Run a trademark search to confirm it isn't already in use.
- Check with your broker to see if you can use the name.

CREATE YOUR BRAND NAME

To create a brand name, ask yourself:

- Do I want my brand to have a founder name?
- If not, what type of name do I want?
- Am I willing to file paperwork?
- Does this name stand out from the crowd?
- Is it easy to remember?
- Is it easy to spell and say?
- Does the name translate well in local languages spoken by your community?
- What's the story behind the name?
- Do you feel confident when saying it aloud?
- Does it connect instantly with your community?

Brand Slogan: Your Value Proposition

A slogan summarizes your value proposition in a neat little package with a beautiful bow.

NIKE'S SLOGAN:

Just Do It

COMMUNITY INFLUENCER'S SLOGAN:

Think bigger!

CREATE YOUR BRAND SLOGAN

To create a brand slogan, ask yourself:

- Does this slogan help reinforce my brand's meaning?
- Does it distinguish me from my competitors?
- Is it short?
- Does it define who we are?
- Does it represent what we do?
- Does it describe why we're essential to our clients?
- Is it timeless?
- Does it make me smile?
- Does it reflect my personality?
- Does it create attention?
- Does it create confusion?
- Is it memorable?

Brand Copy: Your Messaging

Copywriting is so important that I've dedicated an entire chapter to it in this book.

That completes all of the elements of a brand's verbal identity. Now, let's cover all the elements of a brand's visual identity.

VISUAL IDENTITY: YOUR DESIGN

Again, a brand's visual identity consists of its logos, colors, and fonts. Colors and fonts are so important that I will cover them in-depth later on, but I'll cover logos quickly now.

Brand Logo: Graphic Representation

A logo is a graphic representation of your brand. Whenever someone starts a business, the first thing they do is start working on their logo. Are logos important? Yes. Is it the first thing you should do? No.

As I'm sure you've figured out by now, the first thing new business owners should do is learn how to market, so they can make money. A logo is just one small aspect of your business, and if you don't have thousands of dollars to blow on creating one—it can wait.

I made almost $10 million in revenue before I got a logo professionally designed for Community Influencer®. Before that, I just used a simple wordmark, written in a font that accurately reflected my brand. I recommend you do the same until you can afford to do something different. If you're feeling fancy, you can go to a site like 99Designs to have a simple logo done quickly. Otherwise, don't spend too much time, energy, or money on this until you have an established brand—there are other aspects of branding that will make you far more money.

BRAND IMAGE: WHO YOUR CLIENTS THINK YOU ARE

We've already covered brand identity (who you think you are) and formal identity (how you present yourself to the world). Now it's time to discuss brand image (who your clients think you are).

BRAND IMAGE COMPONENTS

How a brand is encountered (Perception)

How a brand is engaged (Interaction)

How a brand is embraced (Emotion)

How a brand is endorsed (Recollection)

Do any of these components sound familiar?

You guessed it. They correspond to the stages of your flywheel!

A strong brand has the power to persuade people to hire you, even in your absence. Jeff Bezos said it best: "Your brand is what other people say about you when you're not in the room." This means that your brand's image has the potential to sell silently on your behalf, which is what makes it so powerful.

Ultimately, if a company doesn't work on its branding, it will become absorbed by one that does (or commoditized by one that doesn't).

FULL CIRCLE

A brand is worthless if it doesn't connect with audiences correctly. It is your job to create a brand identity that resonates. Branding expert David Brier says, "If you don't give the market the story to talk about, they'll define your brand's story for you."

One of my favorite brands of all time is Disney. Not because I'm a fan, but because they do marketing and branding better than anyone else on earth. I love the way the brand is perceived and the feelings it evokes. People perceive Disney as pure magic, and it creates a sense of genuine happiness.

If you tell a child you're taking them to Disneyland, they will remember (and remind you about it daily until they arrive). No one ever remembers that the lines are too long, the prices are too high, the weather's too hot, and the park is too crowded. No, all you remember is magic and happiness because they've built such a remarkable brand.

FORCE VERSUS FRICTION

Apply Force: What levers create momentum in your business?

- Positioning your brand properly
- Competing on value (instead of price)

Avoid Friction: What levers slow momentum in your business?

- Commoditizing your brand
- Competing on price (instead of value)

2.3

WRITE TO SELL

Your messaging matters. Every word you choose should lead you closer to a sale because every word you say either sells or repels. So you need to choose your words wisely—also known as the art of copywriting.

Great copywriting is conversational, simple, intentional, and, most importantly, persuasive. Ultimately, it's the process of using persuasive words to guide someone to a "yes."

"Yes" to noticing you

"Yes" to paying attention to you

"Yes" to reaching out to you

"Yes" to signing a contract

"Yes" to referring you

Writing persuasive copy is like printing unlimited money. But it's an art form that takes time and patience to master. So to accelerate this process, I'm going to introduce you to Robert Cialdini's "6 Principles of Persuasion"[1] and cover them in detail.

SIX PRINCIPLES OF PERSUASION

Reciprocity

Scarcity

Authority

Commitment/Consistency

Liking

Social Proof

PERSUASION PRINCIPLE #1: RECIPROCITY

Humans feel compelled to return favors. When someone does you a favor, you feel indebted to the person—it's human nature. Reciprocity is a powerful persuasion principle used in marketing all the time.

One of the most famous examples is Costco. Costco has made millions of dollars by appealing to our need to reciprocate favors. When you're in the store, you've probably seen them offer free samples to hungry shoppers as they walk up and down the aisles. Costco hopes that you'll feel compelled to buy the whole box once you accept the free sample. And I do, every single time.

---

1 Robert B. Cialdini, *Influence: The Psychology of Persuasion* (New York: Harper Business, 2006), Kindle edition.

You can apply the principle of reciprocity to your copy by delivering something of value. Here's an example:

> ***Learn how to sell your home for more money in less time.***
>
> ***Click here to watch now!***

The goal is to deliver value first, which gives them a sample of your unique knowledge, expertise, and skills. And when you deliver high-value content consistently, they feel compelled to return the favor. In this case, reciprocity makes you the clear, obvious choice when they begin their search for the perfect agent to help them buy, sell, or invest in real estate.

Every day, we have academy members who tell us that they're getting "come list me" leads from people they don't know and have never met. But after doing a little digging, these members often realize that these leads didn't come from thin air. Typically, these leads have been voraciously consuming high-value content from our members on platforms like Instagram, YouTube, or email. These members had given consistently for months and their effort materialized into commissions shortly after.

So, always give before you receive. Even when it feels fruitless—it never is. You're banking massive amounts of loyalty that will pay off soon enough.

PERSUASION PRINCIPLE #2: SCARCITY

Humans have an innate fear of missing out (FOMO). We covet things that are just out of our reach. When something is seasonal, exclusive, one of a kind, limited edition, or out of stock, we want it *more*!

The auction-style shopping channels have made millions by using scarcity as a marketing model. For example, QVC and the Home Shopping Network offer a limited number of products for sale and alert viewers constantly when a color, size, or flavor sells out. When they start the auction, you often think the product is ridiculous. But after you begin to see the quantity dwindle, you naturally become more enticed to buy. (I have several Snuggies and a ShamWow to prove it!)

Another example is Starbucks' Pumpkin Spice Latte. Every fall, I patiently wait for the Pumpkin Spice Latte to return. And once it does, I drop what I'm doing and beeline to the nearest Starbucks. That is scarcity in action!

You can use scarcity in your copywriting too. Here's an example:

> ***This home has the largest lot in the entire community, and it's the only one that also has a pool.***

If you want to sell a home for more money and in less time, master the art of scarcity. Your copy should create massive buzz around your new listings and open houses. When buyers see the high demand, FOMO kicks in, and they'll feel compelled to put in an offer quickly. Scarcity is the sole reason why multiple offers and bidding wars exist. So when something is scarce, tell them!

PERSUASION PRINCIPLE #3: AUTHORITY

Humans tend to follow the leader. This is why we form lines for literally no reason at all. I can't tell you how many times I've seen a line and stood in the queue, only to discover that I was waiting in the wrong line the whole time. We don't even bother to ask the person at the front what they're waiting for; we simply fall in line and follow the leader.

Nike has made billions of dollars using the persuasion of authority in its marketing. The Air Jordan is the top-selling shoe of all time because everyone wants to be "like Mike." Brands use celebrities, athletes, and musicians all the time to subtly signal authority. Some brands are so good that they have signaled authority through the use of mere copy alone. The Apple Genius Bar is a great example.

Apple does all of their marketing well, but they are particularly well-known for their exceptional use of copy. This is why they refer to their technical support team as "geniuses." Of course, they could have used the term "tech support" like every other company. But instead, they strategically chose a word that would signal authority: genius. This is why whenever I have a computer issue, I march right into the Apple store, go straight to the Genius Bar, and do whatever they tell me. It's all because I'm confident they can help. It's literally *genius*!

You can use authority in your copy too. Lyrics and scripts are verbal forms of copy. Knowing how to answer common questions is critical to the art of persuasion. So practice it often! When you speak confidently and overcome objections easily, you'll sell effortlessly.

The next time someone asks you, "How's real estate?," have compelling copy on deck, speak with authority, blow them away with your expertise, and move the person closer to a sale.

PERSUASION PRINCIPLE #4: COMMITMENT AND CONSISTENCY

People tend to gravitate toward what is familiar and what they know. Unfortunately, sometimes it's just easier to "deal with the devil we know" than to do the work to make a change.

McDonald's is a classic example of consistency in action. They've made billions of dollars, not because they make the best hamburgers in the world, but because they make the most consistent hamburgers in the world. Wherever you are in the world, you can walk into a McDonald's and know exactly how that burger will taste. This consistency keeps people committed and keeps them from going somewhere else to get a burger—even if the burger is better.

In fact, McDonald's understands the persuasive power of commitment so well, they were the first fast food chain to market directly to kids. They realized early on that if they could get kids to commit at an early age, they'd have customers for life, and that's exactly why they created the Happy Meal. Love it or hate it, that's the power of commitment and consistency in action.

Humans don't like the unknown. We want to work with and buy products from people who are already familiar to us. Ultimately, no one *really* wants to go with a different agent; they only do because they feel they have a much better opportunity elsewhere. But if you can use compelling copy to reinforce a unique and seamless experience before, during, and after the sale, your competition becomes irrelevant. And you'll have a client for life.

PERSUASION PRINCIPLE #5: LIKING

People are more likely to do things for individuals they like or admire. Elon Musk is an excellent example of this principle in action, which is why Tesla has made billions of dollars since Elon Musk took over as CEO. When people buy Tesla, they're not just buying a car. They're buying Elon. These people love what he stands for, who he is, and the products he produces. So when they walk into the Tesla store, they're already sold.

Mickey Mouse is another example. Although he's not technically a person, people buy from Disney because they love Mickey. But did you know that he was actually designed to be more likable? Yep, Mickey's eyes are strategically drawn to be half the size of his face. He was specifically designed to look more childlike because the human brain is chemically engineered to think kids are cute. So when we see Mickey, we (unknowingly) see a character we can't help but love.

Likability is a powerful persuasion principle that you can use in your marketing too. When you write copy, make it easy for people to like you. There are plenty of opportunities to do that in your agent bio and your brand startup story, brand mission, vision, and values.

PERSUASION PRINCIPLE #6: SOCIAL PROOF

People tend to do things that others are already doing. Have you ever seen a bunch of people gathered together then found yourself pausing in an effort to see what they are all doing? That's social proof in action!

Food, fashion, and entertainment industries capitalize on social proof to drive traffic all the time. Long lines outside busy restaurants, high-end clothing stores, and popular theaters all communicate social proof.

You can use social proof in your copywriting as well. All you have to do is show people that you're working with other people. You can easily do this with powerful testimonials, five-star reviews, and word-of-mouth referrals. When your brand messaging is strong, people will use it to share their experiences with others. Reinforce your copy, let it resonate in all your channels, then listen as your clients repeat it back to you. Use persuasive copy anywhere to guide people one step closer to a "yes."

PERSUASIVE COPY LOCATIONS

Headlines

Descriptions

Subject Lines

Body Copy

Calls to Action

Emails

Website

Marketing Material

Signage

Lyrics and Scripts

PERSUASIVE HEADLINES

Now that we've covered persuasive copy's general principles, let's talk about compelling headlines. The sole purpose of a headline is to get the reader to scroll down and read the rest of the text. If you don't have a captivating headline, no one will even see the rest of what you wrote—that's why every headline needs to be persuasive.

On average, only 20 percent of people even read past the headline. I would argue that's because most headlines aren't compelling enough to keep reading. This is why I spend most of my time writing the headline—to speed up the process.

Luckily, most persuasive headlines fall into one of the following categories:

- Specific or Data-Driven
- Easy to Understand
- Captivating
- Brief
- Emotional
- Shocking

As long as you use these categories as a guide, it becomes much easier to write persuasive headlines that move people closer to "yes." Here are some quick examples:

Specific or Data-Driven

Home Values Are up 17 Percent.

What's Your Home Worth Now?

Easy to Understand

Seven Simple Steps to Sell Your Home for More Money

Captivating

How to Avoid Buying a Property Lemon

Brief

Let's Talk

Emotional

You Are Not Alone

Shocking

The $75 Million Home Next Door

PERSUASIVE CTAS

A call to action (CTA) tells the reader exactly what to do next, which usually comes at the end of our body copy.

So here's the flow:

- The headline sells the body copy.
- The body copy sells the call to action.
- The call to action sells the next step to "yes."

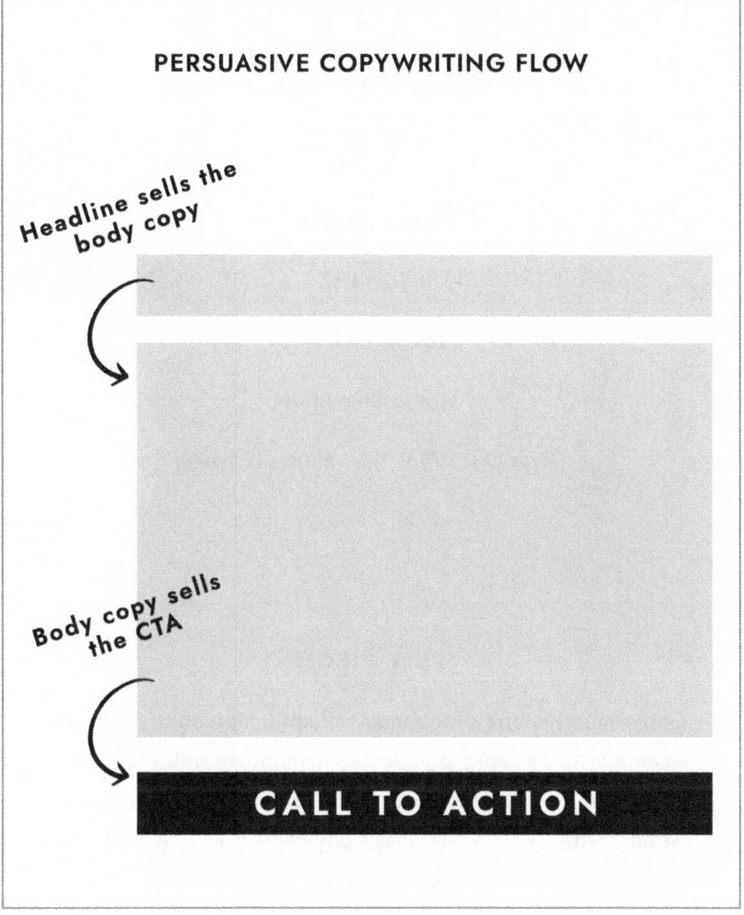

A strong call to action always tells people what to do next.

If you want someone to call you, tell them.

If you want someone to text you, tell them.

If you want someone to download something, tell them.

Always end with a strong call to action.

STRONG CTA EXAMPLES:

Text Me

Message Me

Join Us!

Search for Homes

Get Listing Alerts

Find Out What Your Home Is Worth

FULL CIRCLE

Copywriting is one of the most valuable marketing skills you can master because persuasive writing can guide anyone to a "yes." It may take time, but if you can master the art of writing persuasive headlines, body copy, and CTAs, you can create revenue out of thin air for the rest of your life.

In the meantime, practice analyzing all of the marketing copy you see. If the copy compelled you to take action, ask yourself why. If it repelled you, ask yourself why.

When I was a brand-new agent, top producers kept asking me how I was generating so many leads. After all, I started in a brand-new market—with no sphere, no clients, and no referrals. What they didn't know is that I had a unique skillset that allowed me to captivate, compel, and sell easily. I used

my copy skills to drive traffic, leads, and sales for these top-producing agents. I've now empowered you to do the same.

FORCE VERSUS FRICTION

Apply Force: What levers create momentum in your business?

- Writing intentionally and persuasively
- Writing captivating headlines that command attention
- Writing body copy that creates connection
- Writing strong CTAs that compel and sell

Avoid Friction: What levers slow momentum in your business?

- Writing consistently about topics that don't matter to your ideal clients
- Writing boring headlines that are easily ignored
- Writing sloppy copy that causes confusion
- Writing weak CTAs that repel instead of sell

2.4

DESIGN TO SELL

COLOR STORY

Most people don't know this about me, but I'm an artist. My last semester at the University of Southern California required an oil painting class, and I've been painting as a hobby ever since. But before I was even allowed to pick up a brush, my professor forced us to learn color theory. At the time, I had no idea that this skill would be *so* valuable for me in my career.

COLOR CURRENCY

Artists and designers know that design sells—marketers do, too. We see companies leveraging their design regularly to improve brand recognition and engage with consumers. I love Paul Rand's explanation: "Design is the silent ambassador of your brand."

Brands use color to connect, communicate, and convert every day. For example, Starbucks became famous with the help of its iconic green straw. Apple's white headphones stood out in a sea of boring black. Fast-food chains spend millions of dollars on research and development to understand which colors will *make* you hungry. They're using design and creativity to make money, and you can do the same.

COLOR THEORY AND THE COLOR WHEEL

Color theory is the psychology of color. Artists use color theory to activate different areas of the brain—and this is where things get interesting.

Isaac Newton, the father of modern color theory, invented the color wheel in 1666. He noted all of the colors visible to the human eye and then mapped them all out on a wheel to show their relationships.

Red, orange, and yellow comprise the warm colors, while blue, green, and purple are cool colors. Warm colors communicate energy, warmth, and passion, and cool colors convey serenity, calmness, and stability.

When choosing your brand colors, it is important to follow your intuition. It's a surefire way to stay true to your brand's unique style. What temperature naturally draws you in? Once you know, it's a lot easier to decide which colors would be a good representation of your brand. If you're having trouble, take a quick trip to your closet! Step back and look at all your clothes at once. Do you see a majority of one color? Then that's the color that draws you in because that's the one you buy most often.

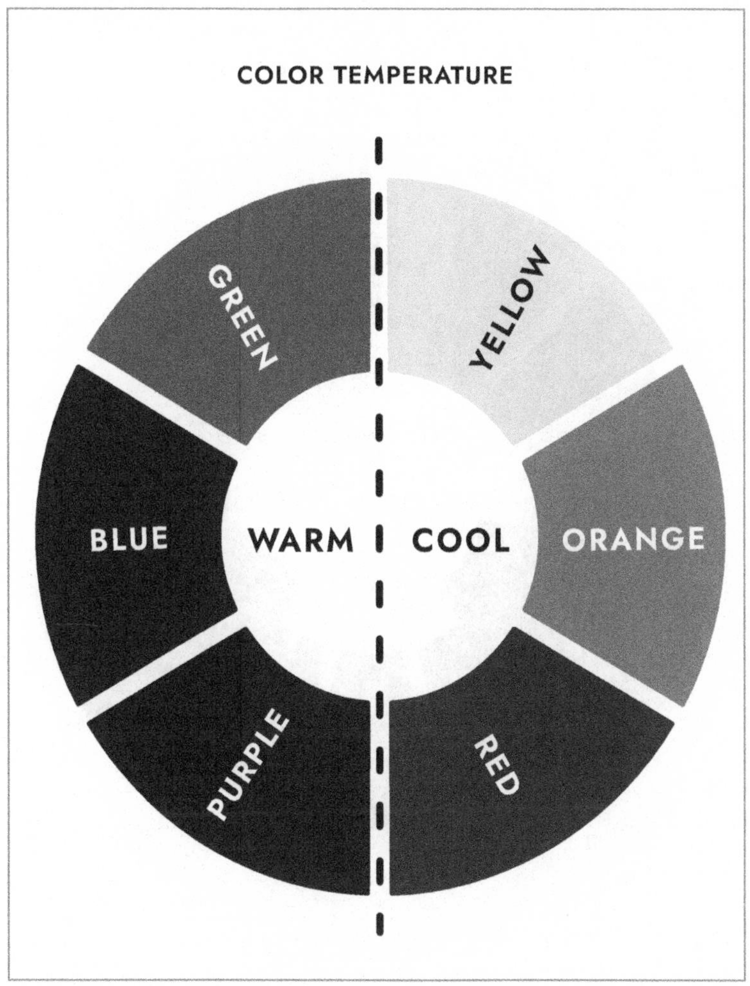
COLOR TEMPERATURE
GREEN
YELLOW
BLUE
WARM
COOL
ORANGE
PURPLE
RED

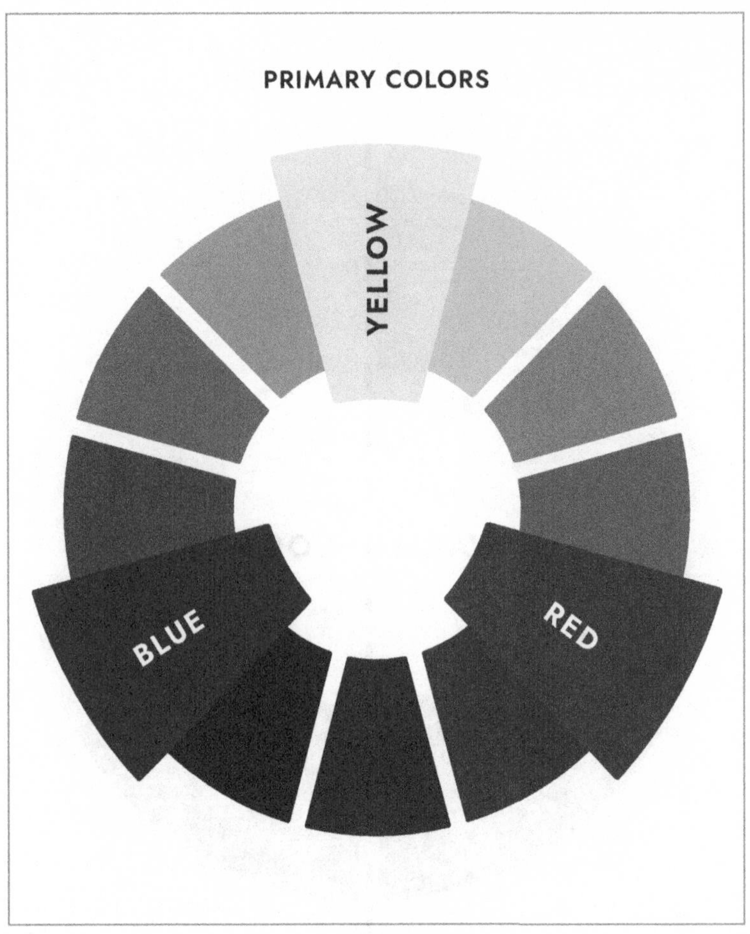

There are only three primary colors: red, yellow, and blue. Primary colors are the building blocks of every other color. So basically, if you only had these three colors to paint with, you could mix them into different color combinations to create every other color on the spectrum! They're typically the first colors we learn as children, which is why they're used so often to market to kids.

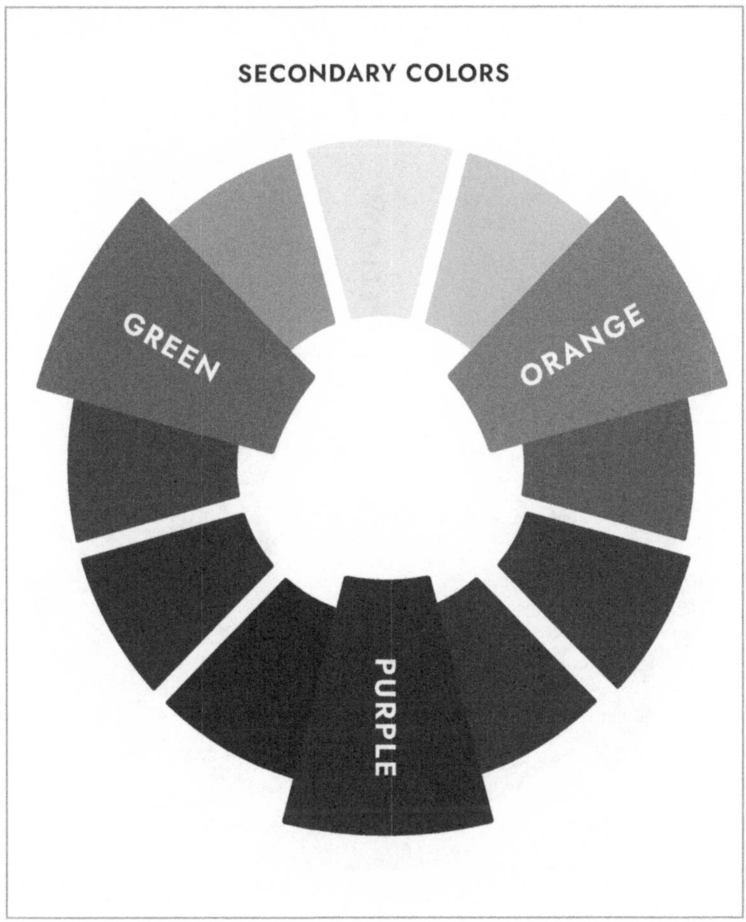

When you mix different combinations of primary colors, you get secondary colors. For example, red and yellow create orange, yellow and blue create green, and blue and red create purple. Therefore, orange, green, and purple are all considered secondary colors.

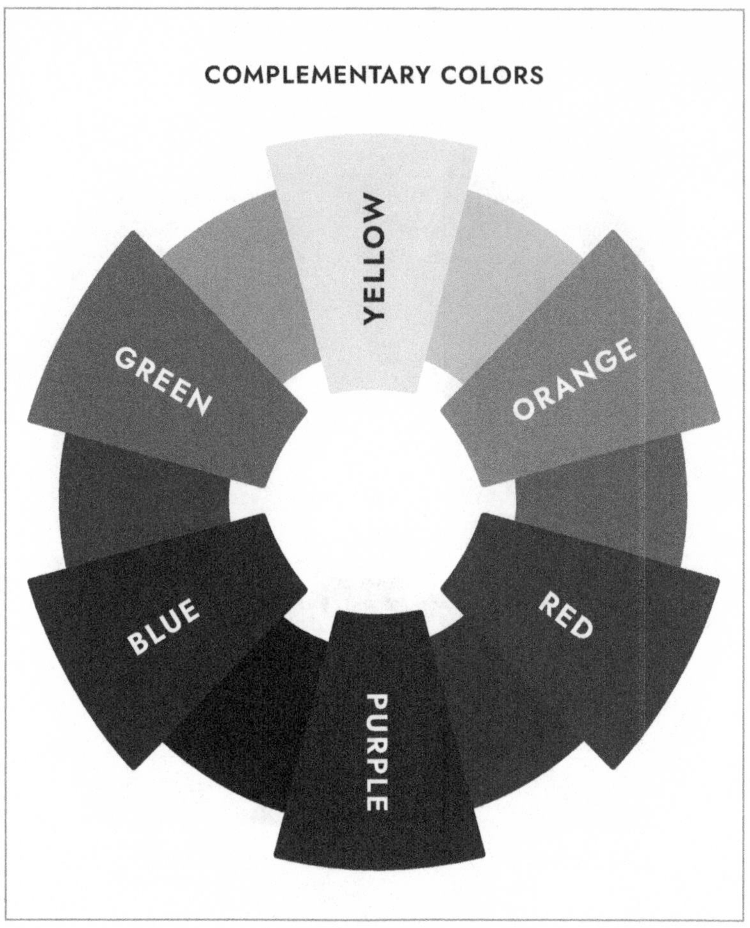

When primary and secondary colors pair with one another, they are called complementary colors. Take a good look at the color wheel above. You'll probably notice that complementary colors are opposites on the color wheel. Red is the opposite of green, orange is the opposite of blue, and yellow is the opposite of purple. When these colors are used together, they really stand out—sometimes a little too much.

When you're using complementary colors in your branding, only use them sparingly, when you're going for high impact. Otherwise, it may come off as harsh or obnoxious. For instance, if you choose red and green, it may feel a little ridiculous—like an eternal Christmas.

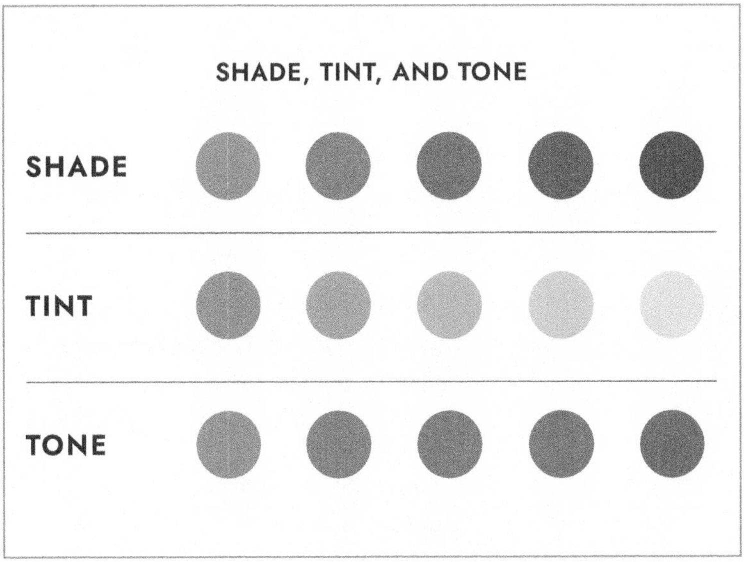

SHADE, TINT, AND TONE

SHADE

TINT

TONE

Now that you understand the basics, let's take it further and talk about shade, tint, and tone. Each creates a spectrum of colors based on the initial color you started with for your design.

- **Shade** occurs when you add black to a color.
- **Tint** occurs when you add white to a color.
- **Tone** occurs when you add gray to a color.

When choosing your brand's color palette, exploring each color's shades, tints, and tones is helpful. Each of these elements lets you see what a color looks like as it gets lighter or darker.

Keep in mind that every single color has the power to evoke strong emotions. Color has currency, because it will either compel or repel. To help you as you choose your palette, here are some common feelings (both positive and negative) expressed through corresponding colors.

COLOR CURRENCY

White
Space, Peacefulness, Cleanliness
Emptiness

Gray
Balance, Neutrality
Dullness

Black
Sophistication, Boldness, Power
Sadness

Yellow
Energy, Brightness, Attention
Frustration

Orange
Happiness, Freshness, Creativity
Caution, Cost-Effectiveness

Red
Excitement, Passion, Power
Anger, Danger

Pink
Joy, Femininity, Creativity
Childishness

Purple
Wisdom, Royalty, Spirituality
Mystery

Blue
Safety, Stability, Productivity
Sadness

Green
Nature, Calmness, Safety
Envy

Brown
Strength, Reliability, Comfort
Isolation

CHOOSE YOUR BRAND COLORS

Now that you've learned the basics of color theory, ask yourself the following question: what feelings do I want my brand to evoke? Then, choose one color that aligns with your answer.

From there, you can choose up to three more accent colors. Limiting your color palette to four colors or less will ensure that your brand stays minimal and professional.

COLOR CONSISTENCY

Once you've decided on your brand's color palette, use it consistently. People need to be able to pick your brand out from the crowd, and that's impossible to do if they see different brand colors every time. Inconsistent colors create confusion in the marketplace, and confused customers never buy. So pick a handful of colors and stick with them.

TYPOGRAPHY

Your brand colors are a large component of your brand design presenting to potential leads. However, they aren't the only thing to consider. Typography is another way brands silently connect, communicate, and convert with design.

Styling your copy makes it even more compelling and accessible to the reader. Text can easily be styled using fonts, spacing, and alignment. Let's explore fonts.

There are three modern font types that most brands use today.

Font Types

f

Serif Font

Has a small embellishment at the end of all letter strokes
Can be used on headlines or body copy
Example: Tiffany & Co. logo

f

Sans Serif Font

Has no embellishments at all
Can be used on headlines or body copy
Example: Nike logo

Script Font

Every letter is connected to another, like cursive
Script is best used on headlines, not body copy
Example: Coca-Cola logo

CHOOSE YOUR FONT PAIRINGS

Now it's time to choose your fonts. Ask yourself what feelings you want your fonts to evoke. Then, choose one font that aligns with your answer.

From there, you can choose up to two more accent fonts. Your fonts will be used in the following three locations, so be sure to choose one font for each.

- Headline Font
- Subheadline Font
- Body Font

Here's an example:

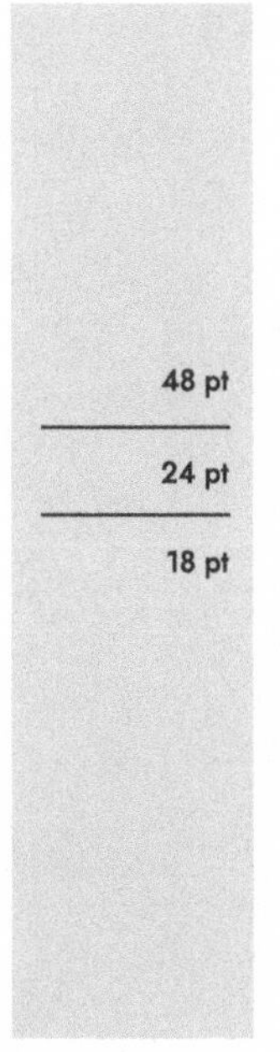

Playfair Display

Poppins Medium

Poppins Light. Lorem ipsum dolor sit amet, consectetur adipiscing elit, sed do eiusmod tempor incididunt ut labore et dolore magna aliqua. Ut enim ad minim veniam, quis nostrud exercitation ullamco laboris nisi ut aliquip.

STEP 3

ATTRACT LEADS TO YOUR LIST

3.1

THE ENCOUNTER STAGE

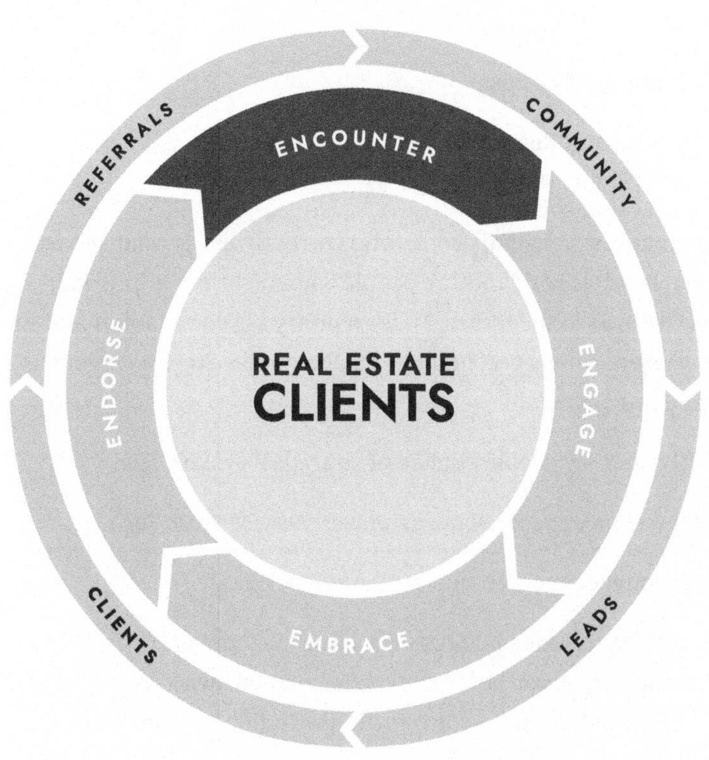

Your network is your net worth.

There's a direct correlation between how many people you meet every day and how many contracts you close every year. The more people you speak to, the more opportunities you have to generate leads and, ultimately, turn those leads into clients!

So your single goal in the Encounter Stage is to meet new people in your community every single day. To start, let's talk about the two different groups of people that exist in your community.

> Your network is your net worth.

Community Groups:

- Current Residents
- Possible Residents

Current residents are people who currently live in your service area. Possible residents are people who might move into your service area in the future. That's a pretty big community! And that means enormous potential. In the Encounter Stage, everyone is fair game.

Will you meet people outside of your ideal avatar? Yes.

Will you meet people outside of your service area? Yes.

Will you meet people who can't hire you? Yes.

At this stage, that's perfectly fine! Even if someone doesn't need your help, they can still refer you to someone who does, so it's always worth having a conversation with that person. And again, the goal in this stage is to simply build your contact list by talking to as many new people as you can.

Luckily, there are tons of places to meet new people today—both online and off—and we're going to cover all of these Encounter Stage tactics in the following sections of this chapter.

ENCOUNTER STAGE MARKETING TACTICS

OPEN HOUSE MARKETING	• Open Houses at Your Listings • Open Houses at Other Agents' Listings
SOCIAL MEDIA MARKETING	• Facebook Profile • Facebook Page • Local Facebook Groups • Your Own Local Facebook Group • Instagram Profile • YouTube Channel • TikTok • Twitter • Pinterest • LinkedIn
VIDEO MARKETING	• YouTube • Your Blog Posts • Facebook • Facebook Stories • Local Facebook Groups • Your Own Local Facebook Group • Instagram • Instagram Stories • Instagram Reels • LinkedIn • TikTok • Twitter • Pinterest

EVENT MARKETING	• Family Gatherings • Outings with Friends • Community Events • Kid Activities • School • Neighbors • Church • Social Activities • Fitness Activities • Meals, Drinks, Coffee • Hobbies • Holiday Parties • Dinner Parties • Pool Parties • Birthday Parties • Coworkers • Past Jobs • Volunteering • Random Encounters • Networking Events • Direct Mail • Signage • Local Sponsorships • Booths at Events
YOUR WEBSITE	• Google SEO • IDX Home Search • Live Chat
ONLINE DIRECTORIES	• Yelp • Google My Business • Zillow • Realtor.com • Broker Directory

Applying these tactics will create force in your business that will accelerate your flywheel quickly. In the next sections of this book, we'll cover them all in detail.

FORCE VERSUS FRICTION

Apply Force: What levers create momentum in your business?

- Meeting new people every day
- Tracking conversations daily
- Being active on social media every day
- Doing open houses every weekend
- Getting on camera once a week
- Attending and hosting events periodically
- Having a website
- Having a presence in online directories

Avoid Friction: What levers slow momentum in your business?

- Keeping to yourself
- Closing off communication
- Not keeping track of daily conversations
- Not being active on social media
- Not doing open houses
- Not getting on camera
- Not attending or hosting events periodically
- Not having a website
- Not having a presence in online directories

3.2

ATTRACT LEADS AT OPEN HOUSES

The first marketing tactic we'll uncover in the Encounter Stage is open houses.

If you're a new agent or if you need to create quick momentum in your flywheel, there's no better way to do it than holding open houses. This is because people who attend open houses are already actively looking for homes. This means that they have the potential to zoom through the outer rings of your flywheel—moving from *Community Member* to *Lead* to *Client* soon after you encounter them!

Since everyone has access to the MLS now, most people who attend open houses have discovered them independently. And that's a good thing! If they found the property on their own, this means that they're not just looking for a home; they're also looking for an agent!

Furthermore, everyone now enters the market as a buyer online, so many of the people who attend open houses also have a home to sell. This means that open houses aren't just for buyers anymore; they're for sellers too! As an agent on a team, I secured one buyer at an open house and because that buyer was also a seller, it turned into four additional transactions for our team!

You can hold an open house anytime you'd like, but weekends are ideal because that's when most people are out looking for homes. I held open houses for two to three hours each when I was a working agent. Shorter time windows allow you to do four open houses each weekend: one in the late morning and another in the afternoon. Yes, this is a big, scary goal. But if you're holding more than two hundred open houses a year, you'll create exponential momentum in your business for years to come.

Whenever I say this to members, the first question I always get is, "What if I don't have any listings?" And my answer is always, "Borrow one." Start asking other agents in your office if you can hold an open house on their behalf.

Start prospecting for open houses on Monday and give yourself a deadline to secure one to four open houses by Wednesday. To do this, open your MLS and look for all of the homes for sale in your area. Then filter the list to show only the vacant homes and start emailing all the agents on the list to ask for permission. (I always recommend starting with vacant homes first because you know the house will be show-ready, and since the homeowner has already moved out, they'll be more inclined to agree.)

On Tuesday, if you haven't scheduled one to four open houses, you can start emailing the agents that have furnished homes next. Keep prospecting for a few hours a day until you hit your goal. Any home you choose is fine—just make sure that it shows well online; otherwise, no one will want to attend in person. I made that mistake several times along the way. But if the photography is decent, you'll drive lots of foot traffic from sites like Zillow and Redfin.

To create even more buzz, you can run a simple ad to promote your open house as well. When I was on a team, I ran an ad on behalf of my team leader for a great home that was slightly underpriced and showed beautifully on camera. People came out in droves (even though it was pouring down rain). The open house was a huge success, with over one hundred people attending, which created a buyer frenzy that turned into a bidding war. One buyer even came with a prewritten contract in hand! Three more buyers submitted offers immediately after the open house ended.

My team leader sold the house in just four days—$25,000 over the asking price. And my team and I got tons of warm leads in the process. As a bonus, because I never gave the exact location of the open house, attendees had to contact my team leader to attend—and we captured all those leads as well.

Collecting leads at an open house is easy. When people arrive at the door, simply welcome them and introduce yourself. Don't ask them to sign in—unless you want fake names and numbers. (I also found that out the hard way after noticing that both Donald Duck and Fred Flintstone were beginning to make regular appearances.) Instead, just tell them about one special feature of the home, then let them tour it on their own. Then before they leave, ask them to tell you what they thought about that special feature you mentioned. Doing so opens the conversation and allows you to speak to them easily before they go. Once you've opened a dialogue, you can start to dig deeper.

When the open house ends, follow up with every single lead. Follow-up is one of the most essential parts of your open house marketing plan. Reach out to every person you made a connection with, and operate in integrity by doing everything you promised.

When my husband and I purchased our current home, we attended more open houses than we could count. It was surprising how many people never even looked up to introduce themselves or start a conversation with us. Many of them didn't even know what to say to start the conversation. And I can't even tell you how many times we walked out the door without anyone even acknowledging our presence.

The sad thing is that my license was in referral status at the time, so we were actually looking to delegate our entire transaction to another agent. I was busy running Community Influencer®, so I needed a great agent to handle the purchase of our new home and the sale of our current home. But because none of the agents we encountered knew how to work an open house properly, we didn't choose any of them. Instead, I chose a longtime student in my academy who took care of the whole process for us seamlessly. She managed both transactions perfectly—and earned just under $100,000 in commissions as a result. Moral of the story: always start the conversation and continue to follow up. (I'll show you how in Step 4!)

Never be discouraged if your open house attendance is low. I know it's a lot of work to curate, conduct, and complete an open house, but it's completely normal to have good days and bad days. If you happen to choose the wrong home or the wrong date and your open house is a bust, keep doing them consistently anyway because there are many other benefits.

The first benefit is that open houses are a great excuse to display your signs in the neighborhood. Whenever residents see them, it creates consistent exposure for your brand over time.

Second, serious buyers are always on the hunt, even if attendance is low. You'll start seeing the same buyers, every single week, at every open house. This repeated exposure allows you to build solid relationships over time. Even clammy buyers would open up after seeing me time and time again. "Hey, Aarin, I saw you had an open house today, so I wanted to stop by." Yes, it happens. But consistency is key.

Third, open houses are a great excuse to run local ads online, which is another opportunity to market your brand consistently. I can't tell you how many people would walk into my open houses and say, "I've seen you everywhere online!" Just imagine how easy it is to start a conversation with a lead you've never met, but who already knows who you are.

That's the power of being virtual in reality. After seeing your brand both online and in person every weekend, homeowners will wander in to start asking you about selling. And buyers will come in to ask you about buying.

Over time, buyers and sellers will move seamlessly through your flywheel, from *Community Members* to *Clients*. So even if one open house is a bust, you still marketed your brand that weekend, and that's a huge win!

You'll miss 100 percent of the opportunities you don't take, so it's better to put yourself out there and miss than to miss an opportunity completely.

FULL CIRCLE

Once, I booked an open house and no one showed up. At the end, I was totally discouraged as I started packing up all my things. But just as I was about to lock up and head home, a woman barged in. Startled, I quickly told the woman about the home and one of its notable features. She proceeded to tour the house quickly, marching from room to room. Then she came downstairs and told me that she loved the feature I

mentioned but hated the home as a whole. I asked her why, she explained, and a great conversation ensued—but I never heard from her again, despite following up regularly.

Then, one day, out of the blue, she invited me to tour a model home in a new-build community. I was surprised but grabbed my keys and raced out the door to meet her. We toured the property together, and I provided my expertise every step of the way, as she marched from room to room once again. She never said more than a few words, but she wanted my help, and I was happy to oblige.

At the end of the tour, she decided to buy the home, and a few months later, I got paid. It was the easiest $12,000 I've ever made. Always work your open houses and never give up.

FORCE VERSUS FRICTION

Apply Force: What levers create momentum in your business?

- Holding open houses every weekend
- Promoting your open houses to get more traffic
- Meeting new buyers and sellers weekly
- Converting community members you meet into leads and clients
- Keeping your brand top of mind among local residents

Avoid Friction: What levers slow momentum in your business?

- Holding open houses sporadically (or not at all)
- Holding an open house without a plan
- Not having real estate conversations weekly
- Speaking to leads without a conversion plan
- Not getting enough brand exposure in your local community

3.3

ATTRACT LEADS FROM SOCIAL MEDIA

SOCIAL MEDIA PLATFORMS:

Facebook Profile

Facebook Page

Local Facebook Groups

Your Local Facebook Group

Instagram Profile

YouTube Channel

TikTok

Twitter

Pinterest

LinkedIn

FACEBOOK PROFILE PROSPECTING

When it comes to Facebook, sometimes people get confused between a *profile* and a *page*. A profile is for social networking, while a page is for business networking. We'll cover marketing on both channels, but let's start with the profile first.

Your Facebook profile is a private place to stay connected with close family members and friends. Here you can receive life updates from those who matter most. You can also post to your newsfeed to keep everyone updated on your life.

By default, your profile is private because it's not designed for lead generation. In fact, Facebook intentionally buries overly promotional profiles in an attempt to create a better user experience. However, most agents don't even realize that there are two sections in your profile that give you the ability to promote your business subtly: (1) your profile cover and (2) your profile description. Both of these areas can be seen prominently by the public, even if the person hasn't friended you. So use these sections wisely—they're both prime real estate. Let's start with the profile cover.

The profile cover photo is like a billboard. So it's a perfect place to add a big, wide image that reminds people you're in real estate. Add a picture of yourself in front of a sold sign, handing keys to buyers, or some other creative photo to let the world know about your business. Just be sure to keep it classy. No phone numbers, no logos, and no digitally edited headshots. Just a natural, candid photo of you—doing what you do best at work.

Your profile description, on the other hand, is another prime area to promote your business. To capitalize on this area of your profile, just write a few words in your description that identify what you do, whom you serve, and how people can contact you.

Most agents don't even mention real estate on their profile cover or description, only their newsfeed—which Facebook dislikes and attempts to hide. But when you take the time to capitalize on both of these high-impact areas, you'll be able to stay in compliance while also promoting your business to close family, friends, and anyone else who may be searching for a great agent in your area.

After you've created your profile cover and description, you can start prospecting on Facebook as well. To do this, just send a direct message (DM) via Facebook Messenger to anyone whom you've friended. Starting a conversation with an old friend on Facebook Messenger is no different from starting a conversation in real life. Ask the person how they're doing and start engaging in small talk.

Eventually, they'll ask how you're doing, and then you can casually mention real estate if it's appropriate to do so. After the conversation's over, be sure to like and comment whenever you see posts from that person in the future. Engaging with their posts is a simple and convenient way to follow up with that person and stay top of mind.

BIRTHDAY PROSPECTING

Birthday Prospecting is a signature prospecting process I teach members in my academy. On your personal profile, Facebook will send you notifications when someone has a birthday. This is a great opportunity to prospect your sphere of influence on your personal profile.

Just send a DM to every person on the day before their birthday (when you have less noise and their full attention)—that's

it! Birthday Prospecting ensures that you're contacting every single person on your friends list at least once a year. It also trains the Facebook algorithm to place you in more people's newsfeeds over time.

We have academy members getting leads, clients, and referrals consistently from using this method. One of our members, Jennifer, got three hot leads from her sphere just three days after joining the academy! Another member, Cari, started the Birthday Prospecting on a Monday, and by the end of the week, her calendar was booked solid with appointments!

Another way to prospect using your personal profile is to follow your favorite local businesses. Most of these business pages are run by the owners themselves, so it's a great way to connect with them directly and build strong referral relationships. We have academy members who've implemented this marketing method and are now getting warm leads from other local businesses consistently. So be sure to follow local businesses as well.

FACEBOOK PAGE PROSPECTING

Unlike your Facebook *profile*, your *page* is a place where you can promote your business freely. In fact, your Facebook Page is specifically designed to help you generate leads and stay connected to those interested in your business.

On your page, you can post updates about real estate and other things happening in your community so they can be seen by anyone following your page. You should also promote other local businesses on your Facebook Page, because it's a great way to build strong referral relationships.

When it comes to prospecting from your Facebook Page, it isn't as easy as prospecting from your personal profile, but it can be done. You're allowed to follow up with anyone who's ever messaged your business in the past. To follow up with any of these leads, just send them a DM asking if they are still interested in whatever they reached out for initially.

For instance, if someone messaged you with questions after watching one of your videos, you can ask them if they're still thinking about making a move and start the conversation from there. If they aren't, be patient. If they are, be helpful.

All of the lead-generation tactics listed above work well, but there is one major benefit to having a Facebook Business Page. Because you have a professional page, Facebook allows you to run ads—the most powerful lead-generation tool available to your page. More on that tactic later!

FACEBOOK *GROUP* PROSPECTING

Local Facebook Groups are a gold mine for meeting new people and staying involved in your local community. Inside groups, you can see updates from local residents, neighbors, and businesses. Plus, they can see your updates as well.

When prospecting from local Facebook Groups, never message other group members at random. First, most of the local groups you join will have rules against it and if the group admin discovers that you're using their group to generate leads, they'll probably ban you from the group. Second, even if the group rules don't explicitly forbid it, most group members won't answer messages from other group members. So it's only appropriate to DM someone if they've specifically asked for help on a group post or comment. In that case, you can send a DM to that person.

But there is one caveat: when you message that group member, it won't land directly in their inbox. It will come through as a message request, so many people won't even realize that you've sent them a message. This is why I always teach our members to comment on the group's thread first to tell the person you'll be sending them a DM soon. Then when you do, they'll be on the lookout for your notification. Once they accept your message request, you can start a conversation with the person and reconnect with them again down the road at any time.

CREATE YOUR OWN GROUP

Creating your own local group is an excellent way for your community to meet and connect with other residents online. The beauty of managing your own local group is that you're the chief of your tribe. So you get to moderate the content, the conversations, and the communication topics. And because you're the admin, you also get to decide who gets accepted or declined.

Some of our members run massive local groups on Facebook and get warm leads every single week from them. They accept all residents but decline local agents, which allows them to become the digital mayor of their town—with zero competition. Leading your own group can be hard work, but I've seen it pay off firsthand.

INSTAGRAM PROSPECTING

Your Instagram profile is another place to connect with family and friends. Here you can see updates from all the people you've chosen to follow, and your followers can do the same. To get the most out of your Instagram profile, convert it to a business profile. Not only will you gain valuable insights on your followers, posts, and stats, you'll also be able to run Instagram Ads!

The best way to prospect on Instagram is to comment on public posts created by local residents. Over time, these residents will see your comments consistently and get to know you in the process.

If you happen to know the person in real life, just DM the person on Instagram, ask how they're doing, and start engaging in small talk—just like you do in real life or on Facebook DMs. Eventually, they'll ask how you're doing, and you can casually mention real estate if it's appropriate to do so.

If you don't know the person in real life, I wouldn't recommend messaging them at random—even though you can. It's really only appropriate to DM a stranger if they've asked for help on another post or comment. In that case, you can send a DM to start a conversation.

To resume a conversation, just reach out to the person again to see if they are still interested in whatever you reached out for initially. For instance, if you messaged someone about buying a home, you can ask them if they're still thinking about making a move. If they aren't, be patient. If they are, be helpful.

7-7 PROSPECTING METHOD

7-7 Prospecting is a signature term that I use to describe my daily social media prospecting process for my members. The process is very straightforward: send seven DMs a day on Facebook and Instagram.

Simple? Yes. Effective? Absolutely.

One of our members, Erin, used the 7-7 Prospecting Method when she first joined, and she quickly got two hot leads right out of the gate. I also taught the 7-7 to Jessica, a new agent, who used it to close five homes in six months!

PROSPECTING ON OTHER PLATFORMS

Platforms like TikTok, Twitter, Pinterest, and LinkedIn can help reinforce your brand presence and consistency so that you stay top of mind. But, typically, they don't generate as many real estate leads as the other social media platforms that we've already covered. This could change in the future as algorithms improve. But until that happens, I wouldn't prioritize them until you master the others.

SOCIAL POSTING

Now that we've covered prospecting on social media, let's cover posting. Unlike prospecting, which allows you to reach people one-on-one, posting gives you the ability to start conversations with people at scale. To do this, post on any of the social media platforms we've already covered—but be sure to post with a plan.

After all, you can't pay your bills with likes, comments, shares, and reactions—at least, not without a strategy to turn those likes, comments, shares, and reactions into paying clients. Social media is not a popularity contest, and you're not posting for fun. I'll show you how to make it fun, but ultimately you're posting for leads, not popularity. So always post intentionally, with a strategic plan.

SOCIAL ALGORITHMS

We can't discuss your posting plan without first talking about algorithms because algorithms determine which posts get seen (or buried). An algorithm is a way of sorting posts in a user's feed based on relevancy. Social platforms prioritize which content a user sees in their feed by the likelihood that they'll actually want to see it. There are hundreds of posts on your social media channels every day, and you'd be completely overwhelmed if they were all shown to you at once. So instead, social media platforms silently determine what you see (and what you don't).

The technology they use to discriminate between these posts is called an algorithm. Algorithms are so sophisticated that they can take hundreds of thousands of factors into play all at once. The coding formulas for these algorithms are highly guarded, but we do know a few things for sure, and I'll list them all below.

SOCIAL POST VISIBILITY FACTORS

Algorithms Tend to Show Posts That...

- are from people who use the platform frequently
- are from people who have a high number of followers

- get a high volume of reactions, comments, shares, and saves immediately
- get a lot of engagement from mutual friends or followers
- get a high volume of video views or extended watch time
- are timely or reference a trending topic
- are from people, pages, channels, or groups that you interact with most
- are streamed live
- are from pages with complete profile information

Algorithms Tend to Bury Posts That...

- aren't fresh and new
- make people feel bad
- get very little engagement
- come from people you haven't engaged with recently
- link out to other social platforms
- link out to your own web pages
- include spammy links
- contain hashtags
- specifically ask for likes, comments, DMs, or shares (baiting posts)
- are overly promotional (when posted on your personal profile)

To keep algorithms happy and your free reach high, lead with relationship content, not real estate content. To make sure you're in the clear, just stick to the 80/20 Rule: 80 percent relationship content and only 20 percent real estate content.

> Just stick to the 80/20 Rule: 80% relationship content and only 20% real estate content.

WHEN TO POST

Every single day, my team and I get asked, "What time should I post on social media?" The answer is, whenever you like! The algorithms don't consider timing a ranking factor anymore. So post whenever you have the time.

Again, it's more about the quality of your content than the timing. These companies want users to have a positive experience to encourage them to use their platforms longer. The longer people stay on their platform, the more ads they can run—and the more ads they run, the more money they make. Social media companies don't make money when users leave their platforms, so they have a vested interest in keeping users on as long as possible—and that includes you!

If you post and ghost, the platform knows you've logged off, and you're less likely to engage with the people who will see your post. So after you post, stick around and engage with anyone who takes the time to engage with your post. It's the right thing to do—and you'll get more visibility too. All of these reasons highlight why posting with a plan is so important.

Posting with a plan ensures that you publish posts that people actually want to see. Over time, you'll train the algorithms, get more free exposure on social media, and build strong relationships online.

DIGITAL ADS

Training social media algorithms is a lot of work and it does take time to get it right. Luckily, digital ads offer a quick fix. Most social media platforms allow you to run ads and some even offer the ability to run retargeting ads too!

A retargeting ad allows you to run follow-up ads to anyone who has engaged with your social profiles or posts. For instance, if you run an ad featuring a real estate market update video, and someone watches it, you can retarget them with a second ad that invites them to contact you. We have members who are getting thirty leads per ad using retargeting ads, which shows you just how powerful they can be!

WHAT TO POST

We teach our members to use a content calendar. A content calendar is where you plan out all of your content in advance. It will keep you organized, on brand, and on track. In addition, it will save you tons of time, so you can focus less on social media and more on growing your real estate business!

Every month, we give members fully customizable graphics and professionally written captions so that they can plug and play. Alternatively, you can hire a graphic designer and copywriter to help you. That cost ranges from $1,000 to $5,000 a month, but you'll have a set of customized, completed posts, month after month. If neither of these options is in the budget, you can use the following topics to help you create a content calendar.

SAMPLE CONTENT CALENDAR

Mondays:

Feature a local business

Tuesdays:

Post a real estate update

Wednesdays:

Highlight an aspect of your community

Thursdays:

Post a sneak peek behind your brand

Fridays:

Post a list of fun, local events

Saturdays:

Promote an open house, listing, or testimonial

Sundays:

Promote an open house, listing, or testimonial

Remember, people only work with people they know, like, trust, and remember. Mixing in a few candid shots and thoughts will personalize your brand and allow you to be more authentic. The more engagement your posts receive today, the more visibility you'll get tomorrow. So never be afraid to post personal things on your business page—it personalizes your brand and people want to know you.

We encourage our members to go on "photo safaris" to get all of the lifestyle shots they need. Just pack a couple changes of clothes, then take some fun photos of yourself around town in all your different outfits. You'll have tons of amazing images that you can add to your photo library. I also do this once a quarter and now have hundreds of photos that I can use online. So just get creative and go for it!

HOW TO USE HASHTAGS

A hashtag is a search aid that helps users find new Instagram accounts to follow. They're like mini search engines. People can follow hashtags, which means that your posts can be seen consistently, even if people don't follow your account.

Although most social media platforms allow you to use hashtags, there's only one that relies heavily on them: Instagram. So that's the only platform that I'd use them on.

HASHTAG TIPS:

- Use three to five specific hashtags that are relevant to your post (ex: #OrangeCountyRealEstate)
- Don't use generic hashtags (ex: #realestate)

If you're strategic with your hashtags, you'll get more free exposure over time as local people discover your brand on Instagram.

FULL CIRCLE

Social media algorithms are highly sophisticated. In fact, they're so sophisticated that they have the ability to learn over time. The good news is that if you train the algorithms to work for you, you'll get tons of free reach and visibility. So always be sure to post with a plan!

FORCE VERSUS FRICTION

Apply Force: What levers create momentum in your business?

- Prospecting on social media daily
- Posting on social media daily
- Training the algorithm to work for you
- Using a content calendar to save time

Avoid Friction: What levers slow momentum in your business?

- Ignoring social media messages or comments
- Posting on social media sporadically
- Training the algorithm to work against you
- Posting without a plan

3.4

ATTRACT LEADS ON CAMERA

VIDEO MARKETING PLATFORMS

YouTube

Your Blog Posts

Facebook

Facebook Stories

Local Facebook Groups

Your Own Local Facebook Group

Instagram

Instagram Stories

Instagram Reels

LinkedIn

TikTok

Twitter

Pinterest

Video is the next best thing to meeting face-to-face. Videos allow you to provide value and prove your expertise. They also give you an opportunity to answer questions and overcome sales objections. They even give you the ability to preframe the client relationship by giving potential clients a sneak peek into what it's like to work with you and your team.

When it comes to video marketing, there are a lot of platforms to post on, but there's one powerhouse that rules them all: YouTube. It's the second-largest search engine in the world and it's owned by the largest search engine in the world: Google. This means that people can find you on both platforms!

For instance, if you created a video called "Top Ten Reasons to Move to Orange County" and posted it on YouTube, people could easily find that video when they google something like "Moving to Orange County." These users also have the potential to zoom through your flywheel, becoming leads (or clients) just minutes after encountering you! Think about it. If someone types "Moving to Orange County," it's probably because they're thinking about moving to Orange County, right?

This is why we have so many members getting clients ready to buy, sell, or invest in real estate ASAP. And because our members know how to establish rapport quickly on camera, their YouTube leads already know, like, trust, and remember them. It's why they're getting contracts without having to go on listing presentations or having to compete with other agents.

One of our members, Wanda, had a couple contact her about buying a new home after watching a video on YouTube. The wife confided that they had decided to use Wanda as their agent before they even met her because they already felt like they knew her. Another member, Karin, has used YouTube to consistently grow her business over the last several years—which allowed her to expand from one market to four!

As a bonus, because anyone in the world can find your local videos, you'll get out-of-town buyers too—which is GOLD if you serve a second-home or vacation-home market. We have a member named Michael who had this exact scenario happen to him. A couple moving back to Missouri discovered him on YouTube and watched one of his videos. Their initial plan was to hire a REALTOR® friend, but after seeing Michael's video, they chose him as their REALTOR® instead.

Another benefit of YouTube is that many of your competitors aren't on it. Most agents don't feel confident on camera, some can't be bothered to film videos, and others are simply unwilling to take the time to learn how. Use this to your advantage!

WHAT TO POST ON YOUTUBE

The best strategy for video is to answer common real estate questions on camera. To do this, keep a running list of all the frequently asked questions that people ask you every day. If one person is asking, there are typically many more. Once you upload these answers on videos, you'll build a bank of videos that can generate leads for years to come.

You can also send these videos to people on your client list to create a better experience for them as they work with you. Anytime someone asks you a question, shoot them your answer on video. You'll never have to answer the same questions over and over again—just send them the video! Video is infinitely scalable from a marketing perspective and an operations perspective. You can easily convert your videos into social media posts, blog posts, or marketing materials for buyers and sellers.

KEEP IT SIMPLE

Some agents spend tons of money on fancy filming equipment, but I don't recommend it. In fact, studies consistently show that professionally produced videos don't convert as well as candid ones do. That's typically because people don't expect to see professionals on social media; they want to see people—real people.

Keeping it simple makes filming fast and easy. If it's not, you'll also be unmotivated to film. So ditch the complicated planning, equipment, and editing. Just outline, film, and post!

I've spent thousands of dollars on fancy cameras, lighting, and microphones over the years. And, honestly, I don't use any of them. Whenever I want to create content, the thing I reach for most is my phone (because it's easiest). If you follow suit, you already have everything you need to start filming amazing videos right now, in your purse or pocket. If you're feeling fancy, you can purchase a few basic tools and add them into your mix.

ADDITIONAL FILMING EQUIPMENT

(Totally Optional)

Microphone:

Record your voice clearly if you're standing far away from your phone

Tripod:

Stabilize your phone, so you don't have to hold it in place while you're filming

Gimbal:

Stabilize your phone, so it doesn't shake while you're walking

Lighting:

Illuminate your workspace when you're filming indoors

HOW TO FILM

First, make a few quick notes about what you want to say so you don't forget anything along the way. Next, confirm that your phone is fully charged. Then, style your scene by removing all background clutter and distractions. Light your scene with natural sunlight (or artificial lighting). Put your phone on "Do Not Disturb" mode so you don't get notifications while filming. Then, mount your phone to a stabilization device—like a tripod, gimbal, or stack of books. And finally, press record!

FIVE-STEP FILMING FLOW

Introduction:

State who you are, whom you serve, and the topic you're going to talk about

Problem:

Highlight common problems related to the topic

Solution:

Give three to seven helpful steps that provide a solution to the problem

Call to Action:

State a strong call to action, so the viewer knows what to do next

Conclusion:

Thank viewers for watching your video

BATCH CONTENT TO SAVE TIME

As a quick tip, you can save time by filming all your videos for the month at the same time. This concept is called *batching*.

To batch your videos, have a few different outfits ready to go. Record your first video, change your clothes, then record the next video. Repeat this process until you have all your videos recorded for the month. Schedule them all to publish weekly until all your videos have been released for that month. Repeat this process month after month.

Batching is a lifesaver. It'll look like you recorded your videos on different days but take you a lot less time.

PROMOTE YOUR VIDEOS ON OTHER PLATFORMS

Create all of your videos with the intent to post them on YouTube because that's where you'll get the most traction. But once you've created the video, you can post it to as many other social media platforms as you want to increase your exposure even more. Remember, unlike YouTube, social media videos are only shown twenty-four to forty-eight hours after posting. So be sure to reply to any comments or questions that the video receives quickly afterward.

If you want your video to be visible for a longer time on social media, you can run an ad. You can even retarget everyone who watched your video with a second ad that invites them to take the next step in their real estate journey. The opportunities are endless.

YouTube exposure compounds over time, so be sure to stay consistent. Create videos every week, and you'll have an entire channel full of helpful videos that can be found easily by your community, leads, clients, and referrals!

FULL CIRCLE

If you're still feeling scared because this is totally outside of your comfort zone, let me ask you this: Is it more important for you to help and provide value to your community? Or is it more important for you to stay safe and comfortable? Prioritize your community over your comfort because someone is out there looking for your help right now! They need you, but will never find you if you play it safe. Success is always found just outside your comfort zone. So get out there and start filming!

FORCE VERSUS FRICTION

Apply Force: What levers create momentum in your business?

- Uploading videos to your YouTube channel consistently
- Creating video content that converts
- Posting videos with a plan
- Replying to comments as they occur

Avoid Friction: What levers slow momentum in your business?

- Uploading videos sporadically or not at all
- Creating video content that's not engaging or compelling
- Posting videos without a plan
- Ignoring comments from people who watch your videos

3.5

ATTRACT LEADS AT EVENTS

EVENT MARKETING PLATFORMS

- Family Gatherings
- Outings with Friends
- Community Events
- Kid Activities
- School
- Neighbors
- Church
- Social Activities
- Fitness Activities
- Meals, Drinks, Coffee
- Hobbies
- Holiday Parties
- Pool Parties
- Birthday Parties
- Past Jobs
- Volunteering
- Random Encounters
- Networking Events
- Local Sponsorships
- Booths at Events

We now live in a world that seems to meet online more than we do in person—but finding ways to meet clients face-to-face gives you a chance to see eye-to-eye. That's because the majority of human communication is nonverbal. When we're talking to people in person, we get incredible insight into the person's thoughts, feelings, and reactions. That's why it's so essential to connect human-to-human. In-person meetings are especially important in real estate, where the client can't shop exclusively online. At some point in the transaction, the client and the agent must meet. So the sooner an agent can pull a virtual relationship into reality, the better. Luckily, there are tons of ways to facilitate this process.

Reconnecting with people you already know, one-to-one, will always be important. There's nothing better than catching up with an old college friend over coffee or meeting a family member for lunch. But when you're trying to generate new leads outside of your sphere, you need to go beyond one-on-one, and plan for scale.

At its core, scale means getting more results with less effort. In this case, the scalable option is to meet more people at once because it allows you to get more results with less effort. If you're going to take the time to get ready, put on your best clothes, and drive to the venue and back, would you rather do that one hundred times, to meet one hundred people individually? Or would you rather do that one time, to meet one hundred people simultaneously? You'd choose the latter, because it requires less effort, time, and money to get the same result. That's what it means to scale.

There are two options for meeting people at scale: attending events and hosting events. Let's dive into the benefits of both.

ATTENDING EVENTS

When you attend events, it's easy to meet new people; in fact, you expect it. As an agent, I loved attending events because strong relationships were forged in person. (Plus, they were a lot of fun!) I've noticed that many of our academy members love attending events too, which makes sense because most real estate agents have a superpower for presenting well in person.

Attending events also presents a big opportunity to get new leads and clients. And as an added bonus, when you attend the same events consistently, there's a huge opportunity to get repeat referrals as well.

Attending events also yields a massive return on your investment (ROI) since the cost of attendance is usually free. Just remember to bring a thoughtful gift to the host to show your gratitude for the invitation!

Another fantastic advantage of attending events is that your lead generation becomes a blast, instead of a burden. It's no secret that parties are way more fun than cold calls. If you can master the simple art of keeping your calendar full, you'll never have to cold call or door knock again!

Finding local events to attend is easy. Your first resource will always be your (growing) contact list. The more you put yourself out there, the more personal invitations you'll get. If you're starting with low (or no) momentum, you'll need to find public events to attend first.

WHERE TO FIND PUBLIC EVENTS

Local Newspaper's Website

Local Bloggers

Local Facebook Groups

Facebook Events

Eventbrite

Local Instagram Influencers

Google

Local Venue Websites

HOSTING EVENTS

Attending events is a great way to start, but hosting events is a great way to scale! You can host your own events weekly, monthly, or quarterly. It's your event, so you call the shots.

We have members who have a blast hosting events like happy hours, dinners, golf rounds, wine tastings, book clubs, Bible studies, hiking clubs, biking clubs, garden tours, food trucks, mommy and me meet-ups, and more. Whatever you're into, that's what you should do!

Again, if you have a contact list, start there. Just invite everyone you know who'd be interested in attending. When I first started in real estate, I was new to the area and had no friends, family, or sphere. So I had to create momentum by inviting people from my community instead. I always held my events at public venues for safety reasons, then promoted my events online.

WHERE TO PROMOTE YOUR EVENTS ONLINE:

Local Facebook Groups

My Own Local Facebook Group

My Website

My Social Media

Facebook Events

Facebook Ads

Meetup.com

And anywhere else they'll let you

I hosted a monthly happy hour that grew from three people to over 130. (If you haven't noticed by now, I scale everything I do!) As my attendee list grew, I was always looking for new venues to accommodate my events. The best way to do this was to leverage local businesses.

Just select a few fun local venues, then stop by around 3:00 p.m., when it's slow. Ask to speak to the owner or the general manager. Tell them that you're planning a meetup and you want to hold it at their location, preferably on their slowest day of the week.

When done right, this arrangement should be a win–win for you and the business owner. First, you'll get a free venue that can hold all the attendees. Second, the business owner will get tons of foot traffic on a day that's usually dead. Finally, if you build strong relationships with these local businesses over time, they'll see the value you're bringing to their business and want to help. Some of the local companies I worked with promoted my events to their audiences, which created a ton of exposure for my brand. Others provided food, snacks, drinks, and prizes—which increased my foot traffic even more!

If you're feeling fancy, you can even ask local photographers or videographers to capture the event, so you have content to promote your future events. This is a win for them, too, because they may get leads from the event. You can even invite local bloggers, who will promote the event to their audiences as well.

Remember, this should be a win–win for everyone involved. Local business owners are a big part of your community, so be sure to build a symbiotic relationship with them. Give before you receive. Our members consistently highlight their experiences at these local businesses—and these promotions drive tons of traffic to the businesses. Our members also leverage their email lists, social media channels, and websites to compound this referral effect.

Remember, we recommended featuring a local business on Mondays as part of your online marketing strategy, and that's a great place to start. Interview a business owner and share that interview with your followers the next Monday. You'll be surprised by how far this simple act of kindness can go. Our members share stories all the time that highlight reciprocity. And, no, they don't do it for the free food, drinks, or referrals—but it's definitely nice when businesses return the favor.

No matter what events you choose, hosting them consistently is the main ingredient in this secret sauce. Your invite list won't snowball unless you're consistent and reliable. It's a lot easier to remember events if they happen consistently. When people remember the event, they attend—and invite others. Also, when invitees look forward to your next event, it keeps you top of mind.

PARTY WITH A PLAN

Whether you're attending an event or hosting one, always party with a plan. Don't get stuck in a corner or a long conversation. If you want to meet people, work the room and be the life of the party.

Also, remember to lead with relationships, not real estate. When the timing is right, you can tell them what you do, and they'll inevitably ask, "So, how's the market?" And that's your green light. Always be prepared with an educated response and keep your business cards close by.

FULL CIRCLE

Nothing is scarier than being a new agent or being in a new market (or both). When I started, I didn't have the luxury of having friends, family, or a sphere. But I did have the internet and a plan. And now you do too!

FORCE VERSUS FRICTION

Apply Force: What levers create momentum in your business?

- Meeting lots of people at scale
- Leveraging local businesses
- Partying with a plan

Avoid Friction: What levers slow momentum in your business?

- Not meeting enough people
- Not leveraging local businesses
- Not working the room

3.6

ATTRACT LEADS FROM YOUR WEBSITE

Whenever I teach this topic, there's one question that always gets asked: "Aarin, do I really need a website for my real estate business?" And my answer is always, "Yes! If you want to STAY in business." If you don't have a website yet, it should be one of the next tactics that you incorporate into your marketing strategy.

Remember, we live in a world where virtual and reality overlap. So your community, leads, clients, and referrals will all research you online before they ever contact you in real life. And if they can't find you online, the only logical conclusion they can reach is: "If this agent can't even market their business online, how on earth are they going to market my home online?" And they'd be absolutely right!

I specifically remember one student who came to me after she'd lost two transactions in the last two months because two referrals from church couldn't find her business online. I hear stories like this all the time. So here's the bottom line: if you don't have a website, you're leaving money on the table.

But not all websites are created equal. Here, I'll answer the most common questions I get on a daily basis, so you can avoid the most common pitfalls.

Can I use the free website my broker gives me?

First of all, nothing in life is free. Using your broker's site comes at a high cost. You're going to run into trouble if:

- You switch brokerages
- Your broker goes out of business
- Your broker gets bought out
- Your broker cancels their contract with their website provider

I've had hundreds of agents come to me over the years who found this out the hard way.

Furthermore, when you use a broker site, you have no control over your leads, data, or content. There are usually no bells and whistles (or they're additional upgrades for a hefty fee). They're hard to get ranked in Google. They promote and brand the broker, not you. Worst of all, they send leads to the broker, *not to you.*

That's the dirty little secret that no one wants you to know: your leads can be siphoned away from you and given to your competitors in the same brokerage. How do I know? Because I work with thousands of agents every day, and I hear about it happening all the time. (It's also probably happening to you, and you don't even know it.)

These broker sites also create dependence, not independence. I'm a firm believer that real estate agents should own, not rent.

Can I use a custom website built by a web designer?

You can, but it's expensive—usually $5,000 to $10,000. There are also ongoing monthly fees and periodic fees that occur every time you change the website. Also, most designers know how to build appealing sites, but that doesn't mean those pretty sites actually convert users into clients. So essentially, you could spend $10,000 on a shiny new website that generates zero leads.

Designers also have difficulty dealing with real estate websites because they don't understand how to integrate IDX Home Search. And IDX Home Search is one of the best ways to get leads and sales from your site.

And once again, it creates dependence, not independence. Agents should own, not rent.

Can I buy a real estate website subscription?

You can, but there are expensive setup fees. You also have to pay costly monthly fees.

And there's a dirty little secret with these companies too. If you ever cancel, the company will hold all of your website's content hostage, so when you leave, none of your blogs, leads, or Google rankings come with you.

And again...it creates dependence, not independence. Why rent when you can buy?

> Renting your website is like renting a home... you have no control.

Ownership and control are why every agent needs a WordPress website. Once your site is built on WordPress, you'll own it forever. WordPress is the gold standard, which is why it powers most sites on the internet.

It also has a repository filled with thousands of plug-ins that allow you to extend the capability of your site. Want to collect appointments? No problem. Want to add IDX Home Search? Sure thing. Want to compile email newsletter subscriptions? WordPress has you covered.

And the best part? The opportunity to rank on Google is high, and the ongoing investment is low. In fact, WordPress itself is free! The domain, hosting, and editor are about twenty-four dollars per month. And IDX (optional) is between fifty and one hundred dollars per month.

If you set it up correctly, your website should be a sales machine. And even if you only got one sale from your website, it would cover the cost of your site for years to come!

HOW TO CHOOSE A DOMAIN NAME

We've found that the most effective domain name for a real estate agent is one that markets the agent's local community—not the agent.

I know you're probably thinking, "Aarin, if I lead with my community, how will people know about my real estate brand?" The answer is simple. The purpose of a website is to get the attention of people in the Encounter Stage of your flywheel. After they encounter your website, you engage with them as your brand. Just like you do in real life—and every other digital channel.

I have a course that teaches agents how to build an entire real estate website from scratch, and the domain I chose to demo for that course was YourOrangeCounty.com. I chose that domain name strategically because Orange County residents care about... you guessed it, Orange County. So when they search on Google for topics related to Orange County, my website pops up. And this, my friend, is an amazing way to get tons of leads, for free, forever.

A few years ago, I spoke with a member named Michael from St. Louis. He was in the grocery store, picking produce, and heard two women behind him pointing and whispering frantically. So naturally, he also looked around frantically to ensure he wasn't missing some sort of celebrity near the celery. Soon, he realized that they were pointing at *him*! The women had seen him online and were excited to meet him in person. Thanks to his website, he gets leads everywhere he goes because people in St. Louis know who he is.

I teach our members to be the digital mayors of their communities. So community members come to them for information, events, activities, outings—and of course, real estate. Some of our members have so many leads coming in every day that they have to intentionally apply friction to their flywheels until they build a team. As a result, they're having more fun, with less pressure, and they're making an impact daily. This is the power of a website that leads with community (instead of commissions).

You can design your website however you'd like, but we've found that a website designed like a local online magazine works best. Your "magazine" should provide lots of helpful information that local residents find valuable.

WEBSITE BLOG TOPICS:

Events

Restaurants

Outdoor Activities

Local Lifestyle

Shopping

Real Estate

These topics are fun for agents to experience, easy to document, and enjoyable to write about. Again, it also allows you to lead with relationships and creates an online experience that your whole community can enjoy. Visitors will come to your site and find value, and you'll get leads, clients, and referrals in return. And because the site is built in a way that's easy for Google to understand, potential clients can find your website easily online. When you design with conversion in mind, your site becomes an automated salesperson that sells for you twenty-four hours a day, seven days a week.

Designing a WordPress website is a piece of cake. Don't believe me? I have a *Web Design Accelerator* course that shows agents how to build a stunning website, from start to finish, in just a few hours—with zero experience. I see agents proudly post links to their completed websites in our online community every day. If they can do it, so can you!

After you build your high-converting website, you'll want to make sure it ranks locally on Google. This process is called search engine optimization (SEO). Here's how it works: First, you create a blog on a popular local subject. Second, your site appears in Google searches related to that topic. Third, people click to read the blog post on your website. Then once they're on your site, they can contact you and become a lead.

There are several benefits to having a website with good SEO. First, anyone in the world can find you, allowing you to reach potential clients no matter where they are. Similar to YouTube, when people search for things like "Moving to Orange County," your site can easily be found—even out of town. If you're an agent that serves a vacation-home market, having a highly ranked website is a gold mine.

For example, we helped a student named Anne build her website. She had zero expectations from the site but trusted the process and did it anyway. Soon after, to her surprise, she woke up to an appointment from a hot lead who was ready to buy a $1 million home in the next three months! The lead said that he chose her as his agent after thoroughly researching her site (and loving what he saw). This lead entered Anne's flywheel at the Encounter Stage, then zoomed to the Embrace Stage within a matter of minutes. That's the power of a high-converting site.

Second, a website is "set it and forget it." If you take the time to create a helpful blog, it can rank in Google for years. So once it's built and starts to rank, you can get leads, for free, forever. We have another student named Myra who created several pages on her site and hit the first page of Google within a *week*! Now, she gets leads and clients regularly from these highly ranked pages.

Finally, that brings me to the third benefit: scalability. If you can get an infinite number of leads from that one piece of content for life, it's scalable. It will allow you to get more results with the same amount of effort—and that's the definition of scale.

IDX HOME SEARCH

People ask us all the time if they should install IDX Home Search on their websites. My answer is always, "Yes! (If you can afford it and are committed to generating leads online.)"

But here's the thing: IDX is not for home search because no one will ever go to your website to browse online for homes—they have sites like Zillow or Redfin for that. So I don't teach my members to use IDX for search.

Instead, I teach them to use it for SEO. IDX allows you to create valuable lists that buyers and sellers want, and these lists can rank highly in Google searches. For instance, if I make a list of horse properties in Orange County, this would be an attractive lead magnet for someone who's looking. You can also run ads to these lists on social media and get an infinite stream of leads on the cheap.

Myra, one of my coaches, got so many leads from one of these lists that she had to turn the ad off. Her flywheel has so much momentum that sometimes she has to temporarily apply friction to avoid being overwhelmed. She now knows precisely which levers to pull to speed up or slow down her business—which is such an amazing position to be in!

FULL CIRCLE

Moving people from virtual to reality is super easy using a website. You can use live chat if you're fancy, but I prefer the phone. Be sure to include your number across every page on your site so people can text you with questions. When they do, you should respond as soon as possible (preferably within five minutes or less).

FORCE VERSUS FRICTION

Apply Force: What levers create momentum in your business?

- Owning your website
- Building your site on WordPress
- Designing with conversion in mind
- Having a local magazine that leads with community

Avoid Friction: What levers slow momentum in your business?

- Renting your website
- Building your site on virtual land that you don't own
- Designing without a plan
- Having a transactional domain that leads with commissions

3.7

ATTRACT LEADS FROM DIRECTORIES

DIRECTORY MARKETING PLATFORMS

Yelp

Google My Business

Zillow

Realtor.com

Broker Directory

Most agents don't like directories because they're listed alongside their competitors. However, there are some pretty substantial benefits nonetheless. First, online directories have excellent local

SEO. This means that your directory listing could be just two clicks away from the first page of Google. Second, because the SEO is so good, these directories also get a ton of traffic, which means more opportunities for your business to be visible. Third, voice assistants, like Siri and Alexa, rely on these directories to pull information. If you ask Siri to find a good real estate agent in Orange County, she'll probably show several listings from Yelp.

Even though many directories show you alongside your competitors, they also provide an opportunity to show potential clients why they should choose you over other local agents. And with Community Influencer® on your side, you'll steal the show. So even if you're not a fan, you can't ignore the power of the directory.

Thankfully, the best practices for online directories are short and sweet: First, complete your profile on all directories mentioned here. Second, optimize these directories with headlines, copy, keywords, and photos that convert. Finally, respond as soon as possible when you get calls or texts—preferably within five minutes or less. It's that simple!

FULL CIRCLE

In addition to being listed alongside their competitors, many agents don't like directories because directories also list you alongside your online reviews—which can be terrifying. But if you're putting your clients first, online reviews should never scare you.

A flywheel marketing model is centered around client experience and shapes every other process in your business around it. In upcoming chapters, we'll talk more about creating an

amazing client experience that encourages positive reviews. This way, online reviews can be an accelerating force in your real estate business instead of a point of friction.

FORCE VERSUS FRICTION

Apply Force: What levers create momentum in your business?

- Having a complete, optimized profile on all major directories
- Responding to leads immediately

Avoid Friction: What levers slow momentum in your business?

- Not having a presence on popular directories
- Responding too slowly

STEP 4

CONVERT LEADS INTO CLIENTS

4.1

THE ENGAGE STAGE

In the Engage Stage, your single mission is to nurture relationships by providing value until these leads become clients.

But first, the real estate industry needs to redefine its definition of a lead. A lead is anyone you know. Period. If they've entered the Encounter Stage, they're now a lead. If you've had one engagement with them, they're now a lead. If you've had one conversation with them, they're now a lead. If you have an ongoing relationship with them, they're now a lead. You get the picture.

And again, your single mission is to engage with these leads until they become clients. The more conversations you have, the more clients you'll acquire. The more clients you acquire, the more money you'll make. There's a direct correlation between how many conversations you have and how much revenue your business makes. So talk to lots of leads until they become clients.

The real estate industry also needs to change its definition of what it means to be a client. The dictionary defines a client as "a person who engages the professional advice or services of another."[2]

This definition means that the moment a lead asks for real estate advice, you should consider them a client. Meaning, if you're talking to them about buying a home, they're now a client. If you're talking to them about selling a home, they're now a client. The second they come to you for any advice or begin to use your services, they're now a client.

I know that traditionally, the industry tells you that a client is only someone you're in an active real estate contract with—but let's face it, if you wait until you have a signed contract to create an amazing client experience, you've waited too long. The right thing

---

2 *Merriam-Webster*, s.v. "client (n)," accessed November 22, 2021, https://www.merriam-webster.com/dictionary/client.

to do is to immediately provide value to everyone who asks for your advice or utilizes your services. If you don't, your leads will never become clients, no matter how long you engage with them.

To provide value, simply share your knowledge. Residents want to know what's happening in the community and potential clients want to know what's happening in the market—and you should be an expert in both.

As an agent, I knew everything that was happening in my local community. If a building was going up, I shared the news on social media. If a street was being repaired, I blogged about detours. If a new restaurant opened in town, I posted a review.

Knowing (and sharing) the ins and outs of my community paid off big-time. I created a name for myself among residents and business owners alike. Everyone would come to me for information. As a result, I had a big influence in my local community. Leads and clients would be blown away by the depth of my knowledge, which allowed me to stand out instantly from my competition—even as a brand-new agent (in a brand-new market).

To become a community expert, study the following platforms daily.

LOCAL NEWS PLATFORMS

Local Newspaper Websites

Nextdoor App

Ring App

Local Facebook Groups

City Websites and Social Media Channels

Local Bloggers

Facebook Events

Eventbrite

Local Instagram Influencers

Google

Local Venue Websites

In addition to knowing your local community, you also need to know your local market. It's shocking how many real estate agents don't know their housing stats. If you haven't taken the time to study real estate, you're not an expert, and if you're not an expert, you shouldn't be advising people—it's out of integrity.

To truly know your market, you need to study a few key statistics. Let's take a deeper look at all of them below.

KNOW YOUR LOCAL MLS

The first step in this process is to know your Multiple Listing Service (MLS). Anyone can do a basic search, but real expertise comes from doing advanced searches—and that requires mastery. Most of the local boards and brokerages offer quick classes for you to level up your MLS skills—take one!

KNOW YOUR LOCAL INVENTORY

Once you know how to search the MLS like a pro, the second step is to preview homes in your market. Buyers now have basic access to your MLS, so they're highly educated. They quickly become market experts and know the inventory in their price range—better than some agents. Never let that happen to you.

To stay ahead of the curve, consistently preview homes in every price range. To do this, view all the houses in increments of $100,000. For instance, if the lowest-priced home in your market is $500,000, take the day to view all the homes listed between $500,000 and $600,000. Then do the same for all the homes listed from $600,000 to $700,000, then $700,000 to $800,000, and beyond. Doing this will give you a good idea of what's available at every price point in your market. You'll have a much better idea of what's priced appropriately. It helps both buyers and sellers who come to you seeking advice.

KNOW YOUR LOCAL HOUSING STATISTICS

When it comes to housing stats, there's a core set of statistics that every agent should know for their market.

IMPORTANT HOUSING STATISTICS:

- **Inventory:** How many total homes are on the market
- **New Listings:** How many homes are recently listed
- **Days on Market:** How many days from listed to sold
- **Month's Supply:** Sales pace
- **Median List Price:** The middle price point when listed
- **Median Sale Price:** The middle price point when sold
- **Price Per Square Foot:** The value of each square foot

- **Tax Rate:** Taxes levied on the property's value
- **Zoning:** Laws that govern how a property can be used
- **Interest Rates:** The amount of interest a lender charges

Knowing your numbers is the key to demonstrating your expertise and the first step to building a remarkable client experience.

KNOW YOUR AUDIENCE

Before becoming a real estate agent, I worked in sales at a popular Silicon Valley startup. I was literally on sales calls every hour, on the hour, for eight hours every day. And I worked there for years, so I've racked up thousands of hours of sales conversations. As a result, I've spoken to every type of person under the sun, and I can confidently tell you that when humans enter into any sales transaction, we typically fall into four categories: *drivers, analyticals, amiables,* and *expressives*.[3]

A *driver* wants space, truth, respect, and strategy. Say what you need to say, then get out of their way. Remember the client I told you about who barged into my open house and marched from room to room? She was a driver. She didn't say much, so neither did I. I kept my mouth shut and let her lead the way—which is why she hired me.

An *analytical* person wants logic, numbers, facts, and plans. In this case, present factual data, then let them mull it over. Don't

3 David W. Merrill and Roger H. Reid, *Personal Styles & Effective Performance* (Boca Raton: CRC Press, 1999).

pressure them into taking the next step. You'll lose them every time.

An *amiable* person wants cooperation, opinions, patience, and fun. Keep the focus on all the ways that you'll help and all the ways that you'll collaborate. They don't like making decisions on their own, so be sure to provide expert advice along the way.

An *expressive* person wants to be the star of the show. They want quick summaries, delivered with personality, pizzazz, and flair—picture Tony Stark in the comic *Iron Man*. To help this client best, focus on how simple, quick, and easy it'll be to work with you—then be sure to deliver on that promise.

Ultimately, when you know who you're speaking to, you can do so in a way that resonates best with that person.

HOW DO YOU ENGAGE WITH LEADS?

Engaging (or nurturing) a lead means building a strong relationship. Traditionally, we're told that there are only two ways to do this: call them on the phone or visit them in person. But let's be honest, no one wants you to call, much less visit. We now have smartphones and doorbells specifically designed to filter out unwanted callers and visitors. This is why traditional follow-up methods, like cold calling and door knocking, don't work as well as they did in the past.

The good news is that, in our modern world, we now have hundreds of other ways to communicate with our leads. Better yet, these are communication channels that people *prefer*. If you want to build strong relationships, you have to learn to talk to people in channels where they'll be interested in talking back.

ENGAGE STAGE ACCELERATORS

Individual Follow-up Methods

- Text Message
- Direct Message
- Live Chat
- Social Media Comment
- Facebook Group Comment
- Handwritten Card
- Individual Email
- Phone Call
- Private Visit

Scaled Follow-up Methods

- Newsletter Email (Email Marketing)
- Social Media Post (Social Media Marketing)
- Blog Post (SEO Marketing)
- Video Post (Video Marketing)
- Public Event (Event Marketing)
- Advertising
- Direct Mail (Print Marketing)

To engage in the best way possible today, you need to know the modern rules of engagement.

RULE #1: VIRTUAL IS REALITY

Modern communication is different from traditional communication. From a lead's perspective, there's absolutely no difference between a call and a text, a text and a DM, or a DM and a comment. To the lead, it's all the same.

I see agents ignore YouTube comments, Facebook Ad replies, and social media messages because they don't count them as "real" leads. That is a big mistake. Modern communication has changed, and our mindsets should follow.

Today, leads can contact you anywhere, on any channel, at any time. Remember, I designed the flywheel as a circle to account for this. If you're ignoring leads on half of your platforms, you're leaving half of your money on the table. When a lead starts a conversation, talk back—regardless of the channel they're speaking on.

RULE #2: FOLLOW UP CONSISTENTLY

There's a well-known sales statistic in real estate:

- Two percent of leads convert on the first contact.
- Three percent of leads convert on the second contact.
- Five percent of leads convert on the third contact.
- Ten percent of leads convert on the fourth contact.
- Eighty percent of leads convert on the fifth to twelfth contact.

That last statistic is staggering—80 percent of leads convert between the fifth and twelfth contact. That means that the vast majority of leads convert to clients only after you establish a relationship. But for some reason, most agents fail to follow up past contact one or two.

They only go after low-hanging fruit (i.e., the leads ready to buy or sell immediately). But if you're only following up with 20 percent of your leads, you're abandoning the other 80 percent, giving them right to your competitors.

I know an agent closing $100 million in GCI a year, but he only works with leads that are ready to convert immediately. He came to me after realizing that he'd have a $500 million business if he had a solid plan to follow up with the rest of his leads. The lesson? Don't leave 80 percent of your revenue on the table. Follow up consistently and build strong relationships with every potential client, not just those ready to move now.

I need to mention one disclaimer before we move on: following up *consistently* does not mean following up *aggressively*. I've heard well-known real estate coaches advising agents to follow up with leads until they "buy or die." This advice is ridiculous. No one wants to be badgered into a sales transaction. Remember, your goal is to build strong relationships until a lead becomes a client. It's impossible to build a relationship with a bully. So follow up consistently, but do it respectfully.

RULE #3: BE HUMAN

Most agents don't realize that leads are trying to get a feel for how you'll treat them if they become a client. But over the years, I've seen real estate "gurus" teach agents how to automate their lead generation into oblivion. Have any of them ever stopped to consider if this automation even works in our industry? (News flash: it doesn't.)

According to the international consulting firm McKinsey, customers base 70 percent of their buying decisions on how they feel they get treated.[4] How you make people *feel* about doing business with you will determine if they actually do.

Real estate is an industry that serves people, and these people are looking for simple solutions to highly complex, emotional, and expensive problems. They want you, not your bots, chats, or zaps. I understand that you're busy, and it's more efficient to automate your lead generation (in theory), but it just doesn't work in practice.

It's impossible to automate real estate lead generation because it's impossible to automate relationships. Your clients are at the center of your flywheel because they should be at the center of your business. If you want to scale through automation, you do it on the back end, within your operations—not your front-end communications. Keep client experience first. (We'll talk more about this in the next step.)

Your clients are at the center of your flywheel because they should be at the center of your business.

4 Marc Beaujean, Jonathan Davidson, and Stacey Madge, "The 'Moment of Truth' in Customer Service," McKinsey & Company, February 1, 2006, https://www.mckinsey.com/business-functions/people-and-organizational-performance/our-insights/the-moment-of-truth-in-customer-service.

RULE #4: PROVIDE VALUE

Your listing presentation starts now. When you nurture your leads by providing value, you demonstrate what it's like to work with you as a client. Take this as an opportunity to educate, answer questions, and overcome objections. It should be an open dialogue, not a one-way monologue.

Before becoming licensed, I attended a party and met an awesome agent. He answered so many of my real estate questions, and I instantly knew that he'd be someone I'd want to work with once I was ready to buy my first home. So I happily agreed to give him my email address. But every week thereafter, he emailed me a list of all the homes he sold. After three months of this nonsense, I happily unsubscribed.

How could we have such an engaging dialogue in person and such a disengaging monologue online? Remember, when it comes to modern communication, there's no longer a difference between a physical conversation and a virtual one. Online and offline are one and the same.

When you're engaging with leads, give before you receive. This agent provided zero worth as he took up valuable space in my inbox. Giving value taps into the power of reciprocity and compels leads to convert to clients. But bragging about yourself does the exact opposite. It creates a one-sided monologue that repels, not sells. So always lead with value.

RULE #5: BE PATIENT

A retail transaction is fundamentally different from a real estate transaction. But for some reason, people in this industry treat them the same.

A pack of gum is strategically placed at the checkout line because it's an impulse buy. You don't need to take a long time to consider this type of purchase. You either want the gum or you don't. Real estate is different. Even if your client is ready to move now, buyers still have to wait for a seller to list the home, and sellers still have to wait for a buyer to submit an offer. It also takes a long time for people to consider making a move. They have to think about work, school districts, loans, leases, moving, and *so much more.*

Every agent knows that these processes take time, but for some reason this industry is riddled with real estate coaches who shame agents into using hard closing tactics to speed up the process. That's out of integrity, and it needs to stop.

Don't ever let anyone shame you for not "tricking" your clients into transactions. A home is not a pack of gum. It's the most important financial decision that someone will ever make in their entire life. Think of its impact on a marriage, a family, a relationship, or a small child. This isn't a game, and we need to take this much more seriously as an industry.

There's no such thing as an impulse buy when it comes to housing. A real estate transaction is slower than a retail transaction because there's much more at stake, and the prices are higher. Luckily, your commission accounts for it, so you can afford to be patient when you follow up.

RULE #6: STAY ORGANIZED

As you implement this framework and build lots of new relationships, you'll need a way to manage them. The best agents organize their leads and track their conversations by using a client relationship management tool, otherwise known as a CRM. Whatever

CRM you choose, be sure to track your conversations and follow up consistently.

RULE #7: LEARN YOUR LYRICS

I'm not a fan of traditional real estate scripts because they violate all the other rules of engagement we've just discussed. They're typically aggressive and mechanical, and they provide very little value to the client. Some real estate coaches have even created scripts that teach agents how to lie to their leads so that they'll become clients. We won't be doing that here because we lead with relationships, not fraudulence. Instead, we use lyrics that will allow you to guide conversations with intentionality and integrity. No matter whose lyrics you use, just be sure to say them confidently, naturally, and truthfully.

FULL CIRCLE

If you asked an expert for advice about the scariest financial transaction of your entire life, how would you feel if you found out that you were speaking to a high-pressure salesperson spitting out scripts? Your leads are real people, with real lives and real problems—help them! When you don't bother to provide an amazing experience, your leads will find a competitor who will.

FORCE VERSUS FRICTION

Apply Force: What levers create momentum in your business?

- Knowing your community and your real estate market—in and out

- Creating an amazing experience by honoring every lead you encounter
- Building strong relationships for the long term
- Using all available channels to communicate with your leads
- Following up consistently and respectfully
- Being client-focused
- Providing value
- Staying organized by adding all your leads to a single CRM
- Learning lyrics to guide conversations
- Recording information that's special to the lead, so you can echo it back and prove you were listening

Avoid Friction: What levers slow momentum in your business?

- Giving people advice when you're not an expert
- Only focusing on leads that are ready to buy or sell now
- Communicating with leads via channels they don't prefer
- Following up sporadically or aggressively
- Being agent-focused
- Sending junk
- Attempting to manage leads on multiple platforms or databases
- Engaging leads without a plan or by using robotic or aggressive scripts
- Letting important information fall through the cracks, so the lead has to repeat it back to you several times to remind you

4.2

CONVERT LEADS INDIVIDUALLY

The goal of following up with potential clients individually is to reconnect with people you've already built relationships with and convert them into clients. For reference, here are the most popular accelerators for individual follow-up.

INDIVIDUAL FOLLOW-UP PLATFORMS:

- Message
    - Text Message
    - Direct Message
    - Live Chat

  - Social Media Comment
  - Facebook Group Comment
- Handwritten Card
  - Birthday Cards
  - Holiday Cards
  - Condolences
  - Congratulations
  - Happy House-iversary
  - Thank-you Cards
- Individual Email
- Phone Call
- Private Visit
  - Pop-bys
  - Holiday Gifts

When you're engaging with leads one-on-one, you don't need fancy automation or bots to convert them. Instead, reply (like a human) with a simple video that welcomes the lead to your world! Tell them who you are, where you serve, and how you can help. This personalized video will stand out from your competitors' bots, drips, and zaps—and allow you to easily win the lead over as a client.

Following up with leads one-on-one is easy. Just follow the Golden Rule: "Do to others what you would have them do to you" (Matthew 7:12).

It's that simple. If you want someone to be kind to you, don't be a jerk. If you want someone to be honest with you, don't be a liar. If you want someone to be dependable to you, don't be a flake. Follow up, be yourself, and create the experience you'd like someone to provide for you.

When following up one-on-one, use the following schedule: follow up once a week for leads, once a quarter for past clients, and as needed for current clients.

That's it! Consistently engage using any channels that the lead prefers until they're ready to become a client. You've already nailed it if you're happy, helpful, and human!

FULL CIRCLE

Remember, most real estate agents learn to use hard closing tactics when engaging with their leads. Not you. I used to know a new agent who was working on a team. Unfortunately, her team used those sleazeball methods in an attempt to convert clients quickly. Although the new agent didn't feel comfortable using these tactics, she used them anyway to pressure someone into buying a home. Her lead wasn't ready to become a client, but the new agent felt pressured to focus on commission instead of compassion. After escrow closed and the dust settled, the negative reviews started rolling in.

The client blasted the new agent on every public platform available. It ended up ruining her reputation (and she's no longer in business). You may be able to fool someone once,

but they'll never use you twice, and they surely won't refer others. These slimy tactics might work if you're selling widgets but not real estate.

These transactions are too big, and the likelihood of success is too small. It's just not worth it because your reputation is all you have. Your reputation is your business, so it's absolutely necessary to always operate with integrity. When you follow up, be yourself, be kind, and be caring. Above all else, follow the Golden Rule.

FORCE VERSUS FRICTION

Apply Force: What levers create momentum in your business?

- Following up using preferred channels
- Following up consistently with leads until they become clients
- Doing for others what you'd want them to do for you

Avoid Friction: What levers slow momentum in your business?

- Communicating with leads via channels they don't prefer
- Following up sporadically or aggressively
- Forgetting the Golden Rule

4.3

CONVERT LEADS AT SCALE

The goal of following up collectively is to stay top of mind with leads until they're ready to buy or sell. Here are the most popular accelerators for following up at scale.

SCALED FOLLOW-UP PLATFORMS

- Email Newsletters
- Social Media Posts
- Blog Posts
- Video Posts
- Events
- Advertising
- Direct Mail

We've already covered social media, blogging, and video at length—so I'll focus on newsletters, ads, and direct mail below.

EMAIL MARKETING

There are several benefits to email marketing. First, because the cost is so low, email marketing will yield a higher ROI than all of your marketing methods combined. Second, it gets more attention than other platforms, because most people prefer to be contacted by businesses via email. Third, email marketing is tried and true, despite other platforms that have come and gone. And finally, email is a marketing channel that you own, which means you control it—unlike social media, ads, or SEO. So even if your social media account gets shut down, an ad platform wanes in popularity, or your Google SEO slips temporarily, you still have a way to reach your leads via email.

But getting your emails into the inboxes of your leads requires both skill and strategy. That's because email service providers, like Gmail, are highly sophisticated. They have algorithms that are highly skilled at placing business emails, like yours, in spam folders and promotion folders. When this happens, your emails are buried, and your leads will never see them. And if your emails are never seen, they'll never get opened.

To avoid this, ditch the fancy designs and stick with plain text. Write your emails as if they're coming from an old friend—not Old Navy. When you send a billion pictures, graphics, and formatted markups, Gmail will (correctly) assume that you're a business and throw your emails into promotion folders. I know that fancy emails are fun, but they don't get seen—so keep it simple.

The second most important measure of success is writing good subject lines, so your emails actually get opened. Copy is king and we've covered it already at length.

The third way to ensure that your emails land in your recipients' inboxes is by not sending spam. Spam is not only inconsiderate, it's also illegal. The CAN-SPAM Act sets the rules for business emails. This law gives email recipients the right to unsubscribe and report you. For every single email that violates the CAN-SPAM Act, the FTC can fine you $16,000. (That's every single email received—so if you send one thousand emails, they can fine you $16,000 up to one thousand times.) Email service providers have zero tolerance for illegal activity. So always follow the rules.

EMAIL MARKETING RULES

- Do
  - Include your physical business address
  - Provide a way to unsubscribe
  - Use clear "From," "To," and "Reply to" language that accurately reflects who you are
  - Email consistently to train email service provider algorithms
- Don't
  - Buy or sell email addresses
  - Email people who never gave you permission to do so
  - Make it hard to unsubscribe
  - Use deceptive subject lines like "Re:" or "Fwd:"

Failing to comply means your leads will never see your emails (at best), or you'll pay huge fines (at worst). However, a good CRM will create ways for you to comply with these laws very easily and effortlessly.

To see which CRMs I currently recommend, go to:

CommunityInfluencer.com/tools

Now that we've covered what kind of content you should *not* send, let's talk about what kind of content you *should* send. We've found that there are two types of email newsletters that work best for real estate agents: (1) the real estate newsletter and (2) the events list newsletter. Let's cover both of these below.

First, the real estate newsletter is a weekly email that educates your leads about buying and selling local real estate. This newsletter does well because it demonstrates your expertise, creates authority in your market, and keeps your business top of mind. Many of our members use this newsletter to nurture their leads, and they're getting clients and referrals from it every week as a result.

Second, the events list newsletter is an email that promotes all the fun things happening in and around town. This newsletter does well because it keeps residents in the loop and provides massive value to your community. To send this email, compile a list of local events on Thursday night, then send it out on Friday.

This method takes a little time to gain traction, but it works if you're consistent. Our members have watched their contact lists snowball exponentially because of this one newsletter. Some of our members now have tens of thousands of people in their CRMs because they provide so much value to their communities.

When I was a working agent, I sent this newsletter religiously—I knew it was a big hit because my unsubscribes were low, and my open rates were high. One week, I forgot to send it and tons of people reached out to me looking for it. I never skipped another Friday, and neither should you!

ADVERTISING

These days, most ads are created online—making print ads a relic of the past. However, I have seen some print ads done successfully in my day. The key with print ads is to make sure you have a powerful call to action that elicits a response. A bus-stop bench with your face and phone number just isn't effective anymore. To capitalize on your print ad dollars, always ask the lead to take the next step.

When I was a private consultant, I helped create a gigantic ad for a real estate agent that was placed in a baseball stadium for fans to see. The ad worked well because we used a strong call to action (text for a free, instant home evaluation). So every time the agent's team played, she got local leads from the stands.

Print ads work well, when done right. But my favorite ads are digital—specifically, Facebook, Instagram, Google, and YouTube Ads. Digital ads are effective because they allow you to target new leads specifically and retarget old leads repeatedly. For example, have you ever shopped online, added a jacket to your cart, but never checked out, only to find that exact jacket following you all over the internet? That's retargeting in action.

Digital ads are powerful because they allow you to stay top of mind indefinitely with everyone who has ever engaged with you online (and off)—for just a few bucks a day! You might be reading this book right now because we retarget everyone who engages with our content. You should too!

DIRECT MAIL MARKETING

Now that we've covered email marketing and advertising, let's cover direct mail marketing. The US Post Office™ has a program that allows you to send direct mail to any local community. You can send between two hundred and five thousand pieces per day per ZIP Code™. Simply print your postcards and drop them off at your local Post Office™ for delivery. They will mail the postcards to everyone who lives in the communities you selected. It's about twenty cents per piece, and you can send them as often as your budget allows. If you live in a country outside of the US, check with your post office to see if they offer something similar.

Again, the key with all forms of print marketing is to make sure that you have a compelling call to action that elicits a response. Most real estate agents send a postcard that contains a list of homes they've sold. That tactic may work over a (very) long period of time, but there are better ways to use your marketing dollars. Instead, send a postcard with better copy that contains a stronger call to action. Ask people to join your local Facebook Group, visit your open house, get a free home evaluation, or attend one of your events. If you don't include a strong CTA, you're wasting time, money, and trees.

FULL CIRCLE

Most forms of follow-up nurture leads individually, but there's an undeniable power to nurturing leads collectively. It allows you to scale your business infinitely by yielding more results

with less effort. Scaled follow-up gives you an unfair advantage in your market because you can connect with more people more often. So there you have it! Use individual follow-up methods to reconnect privately and use collective follow-up methods to connect collectively.

FORCE VERSUS FRICTION

Apply Force: What levers create momentum in your business?

- Scaling your follow-up (when it makes sense to do so)
- Sending email newsletters consistently to stay top of mind
- Complying with local laws and regulations
- Writing great subject lines, so your emails get opened
- Running online ads

Avoid Friction: What levers slow momentum in your business?

- Contacting leads one at a time (when scaling is most effective)
- Sending email newsletters sporadically
- Sending spam
- Writing bad subject lines, so emails get ignored
- Not running digital ads

STEP 5

TRANSFORM CLIENTS INTO FANS

5.1

THE EMBRACE STAGE

Once you've gotten the attention of a lead and persuaded them to become a client, you need to create an unforgettable experience so they stick with you. Unfortunately, most companies are good at marketing and sales but drop the ball when it comes to retention. This is because they haven't consciously designed a client experience that's meaningful to their customer's journey.

My renovation story is the perfect example. When we bought our home, we knew renovations would soon follow. So after we closed escrow, we interviewed a great contractor and couldn't wait to start working with him. We were so excited on the first day, but everything quickly went downhill from there. We expected the renovation to take longer than planned and to cost more than we budgeted, but we didn't expect it to be such an awful experience. For months, our new home was a dusty mess, and every time we asked him for a progress update, he either procrastinated, lied, or ignored us completely. By the time the renovation was complete, our home was stunning, but there's no way we would ever use him again, refer him to anyone, or give him a glowing review—because the client experience was awful.

The contractor did a great job at marketing his services and closing the sale, but fumbled with retention. He gave us what we wanted at the beginning and the end but lost us in the messy middle. When you fail to bridge the gap between sales and retention, you'll lose clients every time.

Don't believe me? Have you ever worked with a client that opened escrow with another agent? Have any of your past clients hired one of your competitors? Has a friend or family member used someone else?

Over the years, I've noticed that most real estate agents design their front-end client experience around their own back-end business operations—without ever considering the client's thoughts, emotions, or needs. It's imperative to focus on retention because losing clients is extremely expensive. Client experience is the biggest difference between rejection and retention; it's also the most significant difference between making six figures or seven.

THE COST OF LOSING A LEAD

The money you spent to acquire the client

The client's current transaction(s)

The client's future transaction(s)

The client's future referrals

The client's reviews and testimonials

Design your processes with clients in mind to keep costs low and revenue high. In the Embrace Stage, your single mission is to design an amazing client experience, so clients are retained and become raving fans of your brand. The better the experience you create, the more referrals you'll get. If you make one client happy today, it can turn into multiple referrals tomorrow. And these referrals will allow your business to grow exponentially. This potential growth is why client experience design is one of your business's most powerful marketing strategies. In this chapter, I will show you how to design an unforgettable client experience.

But before I do, let's revisit our new definition of what it means to be a client. Remember, a client is anyone who asks for your professional advice or services, meaning the moment a lead asks for real estate advice, you should consider them a client. So, if you're talking to them about buying a home, they're now a client. If you're talking to them about selling a home, they're now a client. The second they come to you for any advice or begin using your services, they become a client.

Again, if you wait until you have a signed contract to create an amazing experience, you've waited too long. Start building a memorable client experience now, so they embrace your brand and refer others to it later.

Your clients want an experience, not a service—and there's a big difference between the two. In his book, *Never Lose a Customer Again*, Joey Coleman gives the best definition I've ever read. He states, "Customer service is reactive, while customer experience is proactive."[5]

In essence, customer service is how you interact with clients when something goes wrong. Customer experience is anticipating what might go wrong, then taking steps to ensure it doesn't.

> Customer experience is anticipating what might go wrong then taking steps to ensure it doesn't.

The best way to accelerate in the Embrace Stage is to design a seamless client experience. Here's how:

5 Joey Coleman, *Never Lose a Customer Again: Turn Any Sale into Lifelong Loyalty in 100 Days* (New York: Portfolio, 2018), 34, Kindle edition.

STEP 1: KNOW WHAT CLIENTS WANT

In his book *Duct Tape Selling*, John Jantsch states that "a sale is not a 'finished' sale until the customer receives a result."[6] In real estate, the result would be a job well done. So, in general, what do most buyers and sellers consider a job well done?

For buyers, it's usually getting their dream home at an affordable price. For sellers, it's generally getting as much money as possible in the shortest amount of time. Most clients would agree that you've done a great job if you can achieve these results, but knowing what clients want is only the first step when creating a fantastic client experience.

STEP 2: EXPRESS GRATITUDE

Most businesses never bother to thank their customers for doing business with them. In a service-based business, that's a death knell. Instead, always show gratitude to every person who chooses you. It solidifies the relationship and builds a broader moat between you and your competitors. Showing your appreciation can be as easy as dropping a handwritten card in the mail or personally at the door. If you're feeling fancy, you could send a celebratory welcome video featuring you and your team.

Whatever you decide, make it clear that you care. Your new clients probably had hundreds of agents to choose from, but they chose you. And that event should be celebrated and commemorated with the client.

---

6 John Jantsch, *Duct Tape Selling: Think like a Marketer—Sell like a Superstar* (New York: Portfolio, 2014), 170.

STEP 3: ANTICIPATE AND ADDRESS ROADBLOCKS

The third step to creating your one-of-a-kind client experience is anticipating and addressing potential roadblocks. When businesses fail to build thorough processes to manage fear and doubt, clients create distance and look for ways to leave. That's why we have to anticipate everything that could go wrong and actively fortify the business against them. Remember, client experience is proactive, not reactive.

If we know that most clients will only conduct a handful of real estate transactions in their entire lives, we should also know that they'll have a certain amount of inherent anxiety accompanying each transaction. Since this uncertainty is an inevitable roadblock to the sale, we need to stop ignoring it and proactively address it.

The first roadblock to address is *buyer's remorse*. As you know, in real estate, there's a long delay between when a person decides to work with you and when they get a result. The moment that this relationship starts, every interaction with you, good or bad, is tallied up in the client's mind. As these tallies increase, their significance begins to weigh heavily on the scale of client experience. In the beginning, the client is excited, and emotions are running high. However, once the initial dopamine decreases in the brain, the initial excitement does too. At that point, the client begins to recede into doubt—otherwise known as buyer's remorse. (And yes, it can still occur, even if your clients haven't signed on the dotted line or opened escrow.)

Making big purchases and long-term commitments can easily trigger buyer's remorse, making it one of the biggest roadblocks before closing. To mitigate buyer's remorse, simply acknowledge it. Then calm their fears through confirmation by reminding them that they've made a great decision to work with you.

Providing confirmation can be done easily by sending them evidence of all the successful transactions you've closed in the past, the happy clients you've helped, or the supportive team you've built. Try arming them with a simple video, document, or marketing resource. Once they have undeniable proof, it's easy to manage buyer's remorse.

The second roadblock to address is the *awkward transition*. Have you ever made a big purchase with a salesperson, then immediately been shoved off to an account manager? Typically, the new account manager has no idea who you are, knows nothing about your account, and sometimes doesn't even seem to care. You've built tons of rapport with the salesperson, and now you have to explain your entire history all over again with an apathetic account manager. So what happened to the salesperson? The hoopla? The excitement? The celebration?

This happened to me once when I transferred to a new brokerage. The recruiting process was all fun and games until they made the "sale." Then, as soon as I made the verbal commitment to join the brokerage, the team leader shoved me off to an administrator who made me sit alone in a dark, dingy room, filling out paperwork for hours. A few weeks later, I saw the team leader in the hall, and she didn't even remember my name. Needless to say, I moved on from that brokerage.

Awkward transitions regularly happen in real estate because you work with so many people during the sale. You have lenders, vendors, title companies, transaction coordinators, brokers, lawyers, inspectors, appraisers, assistants, escrow officers, and other agents. If you don't finesse these interactions carefully, remorse will creep in. Instead, proactively introduce these new faces to your clients. Whenever possible, prep your extended team members by giving them any relevant information that would ensure a smooth transition for the client. You also need to prep your clients by doing the same. These introductions help manage fear and mitigate remorse.

STEP 4: MAP THE CLIENT JOURNEY

Real estate transactions are overwhelming for new clients. They have to quickly familiarize themselves with the market and all the processes, programs, tools, players, and paperwork that come with the transaction. When you map the client's journey, you're helping the client quickly orient themself and navigate to reach their destination smoothly. Essentially, the client journey map shows them where they are now, where their destination will be, and every milestone in between.

In the next two chapters, I'll show you how to create a client journey map for both buyers and sellers. Of course, designing an amazing client experience will always be a work in progress, but these processes will help you build a strong foundation.

FULL CIRCLE

Billionaire Charlie Munger often says that in order to keep your competition at bay, you need to build a wider moat. Thoughtfully designing an amazing client experience is not only a strategic marketing strategy, it's also a strategic offensive strategy. Other agents can copy your marketing, branding, or messaging, but they can't copy your client experience, making it one of the best moats you can build between you and your competitors.

FORCE VERSUS FRICTION

Apply Force: What levers create momentum in your business?

- Being proactive, by focusing on client experience
- Bridging the gap between sales and retention
- Building processes that result in retention
- Anticipating what could go wrong and addressing it preemptively
- Expressing gratitude
- Navigating transactions smoothly by using a client journey map

Avoid Friction: What levers slow momentum in your business?

- Being reactive, by focusing on customer service
- Failing to bridge the gap between sales and retention
- Building processes that result in rejection
- Allowing things to go wrong, then addressing them subsequently
- Expressing thanklessness
- Allowing clients to traverse transactions without a guide

5.2

DESIGN AN AMAZING BUYER EXPERIENCE

In the previous chapter, you learned the four steps that allow you to design an amazing client experience:

- Step 1: Know What Clients Want
- Step 2: Express Gratitude
- Step 3: Anticipate and Address Roadblocks
- Step 4: Map the Buyer's Journey

In this step, we will take a deeper dive into mapping the client's journey by identifying critical milestones.

BUYER'S JOURNEY MILESTONES

1. Presentation
2. Exploration
3. Negotiation
4. Transaction
5. Celebration
6. Evaluation
7. Communication

MILESTONE #1: PRESENTATION

Presentation is the first step in the buyer's journey and the perfect opportunity to educate your buyers about the buying process. Even if your buyers have bought several homes in the past, the market changes daily, so make sure they're prepared and up to speed. The easiest way to educate them is to create a buyer's presentation and walk them through it.

BUYER'S PRESENTATION CONTENTS

- **Buyer's Journey Map:** A visual representation of the client's journey that orients them quickly and allows them to navigate the seven milestones of the transaction smoothly
- **Welcome Kit:** Provides clarity and mitigates uncertainty

by outlining who's on your team, what their responsibilities are, and how to contact them

- **Buyer Questionnaire:** A survey that allows you to capture what's important to the client so you can keep their home search relevant
- **Escrow Timeline:** A list of important dates to keep your buyers on track, up to date, and in the loop
- **Benefits of Owning a Home:** A list of benefits that will keep your buyer's eye on the prize as they work toward the Transaction Milestone
- **Trusted Vendors:** A directory of your favorite vendors so your buyers know who to call if they need to make any repairs to their new home
- **Real Estate Glossary:** A list of defined industry terms that your buyers can easily understand
- **Agent Evaluation:** A form that allows your buyers to evaluate your services and give you feedback so that you can improve

MILESTONE #2: EXPLORATION

Exploration is the second step in the buyer's journey. Touring homes is the most exciting part of the home-buying process, but nothing loses a buyer's interest faster than showing homes that aren't relevant. It communicates that you're not listening to their needs. Instead, have the buyers complete an initial questionnaire as part of their onboarding process and refer to it often.

Once you understand what your buyers want, it's time to tour some homes. I've learned the hard way that three to four homes is the magic number. Anything less than that doesn't allow you to spend enough time together to build rapport. Anything more than that turns into an overwhelming chore. So keep your home search relevant and prioritized. Every time you tour a home together, ask what features they liked (and didn't), then update your buyer's questionnaire.

Finally, if your buyer is out of town or unavailable, make it easy, and tour the property on their behalf. You can take photos, notes, or even live videos so the buyer can come along for the virtual ride. Then, keep touring homes, updating their questionnaire, and applying your market knowledge, so you can seamlessly guide clients to their dream home.

MILESTONE #3: NEGOTIATION

Negotiation is the third step in the buyer's journey. Remember, the thing that buyers ultimately want most is to purchase their dream home. If you can make their dream a reality, it will have the biggest impact on their client experience with you. And it all starts with the art of negotiation.

To negotiate the best terms for your buyer, you need to know the contract, inside and out. If you're new, find a mentor to help you. A mentor will usually take a small percentage of your commission, but consider it a valuable investment in your education. One small mistake can equate to thousands of dollars lost and many hours wasted, so you need to get the contract right. If you get it right you'll create that incredible experience, but if you get it wrong you'll create an awful experience—so know your contract. Your reputation (and future referrals) depend on it.

The first way to open negotiations in a power position is to write a competitive offer. If your buyer gets their dream home because you took the time to compose the perfect proposal, they'll rave about your business for years to come!

HOW TO WRITE A COMPETITIVE OFFER

- Pay close attention to the MLS instructions.
- Always assume multiple offers.
- Attach the preapproval letter to the offer.
- Add proof of funds to the offer (if allowed).
- Contact the listing agent before you send your offer.
- Write a simple, clean, organized offer.
- Confirm that the sellers received your offer.
- Be friendly with the listing agent.
- Make things simple.
- Be super easy to work with.

Sometimes, inventory is low and demand is high. You'll need to get even more creative to get your offers noticed when this happens. If you can gain favor with the home sellers and ultimately seal the deal, your buyers will win every time.

HOW TO SWEETEN THE DEAL

- Build rapport with the listing agent.
- Get creative with your offer price.
- Offer to pay cash.
- Choose a reputable lender.
- Increase the earnest money.
- Let the buyer waive the home warranty.
- Pay for the seller's HOA costs.
- Accommodate the seller's closing needs.
- Accommodate the seller's occupancy needs.
- Offer a free leaseback, if it helps the seller.
- Limit the number of days for inspections.
- Waive inspections.
- Get a preunderwriting letter.
- Let the buyer write a letter to the seller (be sure to comply with Fair Housing).

Your buyer may not know about all these ways to make their offer stand out from the crowd. Giving them options shows that you're getting creative, thinking outside of the box, and negotiating well on their behalf. If you write a competitive offer that gets your buyers into their dream home, you'll create a client experience they'll never forget.

MILESTONE #4: TRANSACTION

The transaction is the fourth step in the buyer's journey. All clients have a fear of the unknown. When you fail to keep them updated, doubt and uncertainty creep in and they'll always assume the worst.

Keep your buyers in the know by updating them consistently during escrow to avoid this. You do this every day, but a buyer may only do this a handful of times in their entire life, so be sure you are their biggest advocate and keep them in the loop. There are several software tools that can automate this whole process for you. All you have to do is enter your key contract dates, and then it will email a digital timeline that's super easy to follow. If you're working with a transaction coordinator, be sure to add them to the tool as well, so they can update the timeline as they go.

To further eliminate the potential for fear and uncertainty, be available for all questions, inspections, and appraisals. Honesty and accountability are two major ingredients to creating an outstanding client experience. There are no perfect real estate transactions. When transactions go awry, be honest. When you or someone on your team drops the ball, take accountability. As long as you're transparent and accountable with your buyers, they'll understand when things don't work out—even if they are upset. If they find out later, it will ruin the entire experience you've worked so hard to create for them.

MILESTONE #5: CELEBRATION

Celebration is the fifth step in the buyer's journey. The best part of the buyer experience is handing them the keys on closing day! Closing on the house is a major milestone that should be celebrated, and you should go out of your way to commemorate it.

Get creative and go all out! Just be sure to comply with your local gifting regulations.

MILESTONE #6: EVALUATION

Evaluation is the sixth step in the buyer's journey. Unfortunately, most businesses never survey their clients in an attempt to avoid negative feedback. Think bigger!

Negative feedback shows where you need to eliminate more friction. Positive feedback shows where you can apply more force. Both activities accelerate your flywheel and allow your business to gain more momentum. Always collect client feedback consistently to improve your processes, procedures, programs, and people. Be transparent with your clients from the very beginning and tell them you'll be requesting an evaluation of your services in the end. Do this by showing them your evaluation form and pointing out all the areas where you'll be asking for feedback. Ultimately, if you collect negative feedback privately, you'll get less negative feedback publicly.

MILESTONE #7: COMMUNICATION

Communication is the seventh step in the buyer's journey. It's crucial to stay in touch with past clients—I can't emphasize that enough. This milestone solidifies it as part of the buyer's journey and prepares your clients for future contact. Again, reach out to all of your past clients once a quarter. This is the magic number to keep you top of mind to generate more referrals.

FULL CIRCLE

In 2020, my husband and I sold a home. Because there was an extreme housing shortage during COVID, we got multiple offers. Negotiations with the other agents were intense, but we ultimately decided to go with the highest bidder—which we immediately regretted.

Their agent's idea of creating a remarkable buyer experience was to offer $15,000 over asking (to get the offer accepted), then swoop in with $15,000 worth of repairs (to bring the price back down). He sent us a bulleted list of forty-seven items that "needed" to be repaired to accomplish this goal. When we got the list of repairs, I looked at my husband in shock. Our home was immaculate—but even if it wasn't, I had never heard of any buyer sending a list that long. Soon after that, our shock turned into anger.

On general principle, I declined everything on the list within minutes. (For the record, offending the sellers is the worst negotiation strategy in the world.) A day later, they revised their list of repairs and asked for just thirty-seven things to be repaired.

We declined.

The day after that, they revised the list again, asking for only twenty-seven things to be repaired.

We declined again.

This time, we made it crystal clear that we would not repair anything and that if they didn't want the house, they should move on. The home closed quickly after that. Unfortunately,

the buyers got the raw end of the deal because their agent decided to run a game that we weren't interested in playing.

This example was extreme, but agents do sleazy things to get ahead all the time (and I'm sure you've seen similar sleazy tactics in your experience as well). The moral of the story? When designing your exceptional buyer experience, keep it classy.

FORCE VERSUS FRICTION

Apply Force: What levers create momentum in your business?

- Educating your buyers
- Showing three to four relevant homes at a time
- Writing competitive offers
- Keeping buyers up to date and in the loop during escrow
- Being available
- Being honest
- Being accountable
- Celebrating with your clients after you hand over the keys
- Requesting feedback from buyers so you can improve
- Following up with past buyers once a quarter to stay top of mind

Avoid Friction: What levers slow momentum in your business?

- Keeping buyers in the dark
- Showing too many homes, too few homes, or irrelevant homes
- Writing offers that are sloppy, incomplete, or unorganized
- Not keeping buyers up to date and in the loop during escrow
- Being unavailable

- Being dishonest
- Being unaccountable
- Failing to commemorate closing day with your clients
- Not requesting feedback from buyers so you can improve
- Failing to follow up with past buyers once a quarter to stay top of mind

5.3

DESIGN AN AMAZING SELLER EXPERIENCE

In the previous chapter, you learned about each of the seven milestones in the buyer's journey. In this chapter, we're going to take a deeper dive into the seller's journey.

SELLER'S JOURNEY MILESTONES

1. Presentation
2. Promotion
3. Negotiation

4. Transaction
5. Compensation
6. Evaluation
7. Communication

MILESTONE #1: PRESENTATION

Presentation is the first step in the seller's journey and typically that begins with some sort of listing presentation.

Traditionally, the listing presentation went a little something like this: the listing agent would blast into the home, take a quick look around, plop down at the kitchen table, slam a bunch of papers down, and proceed with the performance of a lifetime—literally. I've heard everything from agents demanding glasses of water (as a power play) to presenting inflated numbers to trick people into working with them to even promising to buy the home if it doesn't sell (at a deeply discounted rate, of course).

This dog and pony show no longer works. In a modern world, your listing presentation started eighteen months ago. If you're marketing correctly, sellers should already know, like, trust, and remember you before they even contact you. This is why our members rarely go on traditional listing appointments anymore.

When our members arrive at the property, they're usually presenting simple logistics (not a magic show). However, you still need a way to convey your value and manage seller expectations, which is what you should include in a modern listing presentation.

THE MODERN LISTING PRESENTATION CONTENTS

- **Seller's Journey Map:** A visual representation of the client's journey that orients them quickly and allows them to navigate the seven milestones of the transaction smoothly
- **Welcome Kit:** Provides clarity and mitigates uncertainty by outlining who's on your team, what their responsibilities are, and how to contact them
- **Your Marketing Strategy:**
    - Home Staging
    - Photography
    - Videography
    - Drone Footage
    - Online Marketing
    - Open House Events
    - Direct Mail Campaigns
    - Listing Syndication
    - Signage
    - Strategic Pricing
- **Seller Questionnaire:** A survey that allows you to capture important features about the home so that you can optimize your MLS listing
- **Home Staging Checklist:** A list of all the ways a home can present well online, so it drives tons of traffic and sells for more money in less time

- **Trusted Vendors:** A directory of your favorite vendors so your clients know who to call if they need to make any repairs to the home
- **Key Contract Dates:** A list of important dates to keep your sellers on track, up to date, and in the loop
- **Real Estate Glossary:** A list of defined industry terms that your sellers can easily understand
- **Agent Evaluation:** A form that allows your sellers to evaluate your services and give you feedback so that you can improve

Again, a seller's goal will always be to sell the home for as much money as possible in as little time as possible. Once you've clearly communicated how you can do that, your listing appointment should be a breeze—especially if they've already gotten to know you as they progressed through the other stages of your flywheel.

MILESTONE #2: PROMOTION

Promotion is the second step in the seller's journey. Every seller wants to get maximum exposure and traffic so their home gets sold quickly, right? Well, the secret sauce for selling any home fast comes down to three ingredients: (1) pricing the home strategically, (2) presenting the home well online, and (3) having a modern marketing plan. Let's dive into each one of these ingredients together.

First, strategic pricing ultimately comes back to knowing your market. We all know that if the home is priced too high, it will sit on the market forever. Therefore, knowing your market is the first step in the pricing process. The second is being strategic. Strategic pricing can drive even more traffic when done right, making it a powerful marketing tool. For instance, if you price the home just under its actual value, you'll drive tons of traffic, and bidding wars often ensue—and a bidding war can drive the price up far higher than the actual list price.

Another way to drive more traffic is to price by level. What this means is if the vast majority of people in your market are looking for homes priced lower than $800,000, search algorithms will only show homes up to $799,999—so pricing a home just $1 more, at $800,000, means the vast majority of buyers in your market will never even see it.

Great listing agents know how to price homes accurately and strategically. So be sure to do the same.

The second ingredient great listing agents utilize is the art of presenting the home online. These days, buyers look for homes based on the quality of the photos. If you want to drive a ton of traffic to your listing, step up your photo game. Always hire a professional photographer to shoot and edit all of your photos. Today, buyers expect to see big, beautiful, bright images. If you fail to deliver, people will scroll right past your listing.

Consider videography and drone footage if the house is large. And finally, if you want all of the photos to really shine, stage the home appropriately. Photography, videos, aerial footage, and home staging are all used by top producers to make their listings shine online. They use them strategically to drive more traffic, buyers, and ultimately, offers, making sellers very happy!

The third ingredient is an airtight marketing plan. We've already done a deep dive into marketing and advertising when we covered the Encounter Stage. You can apply many of the strategies you're already using to market your business to your listings. But I want to add a few additional strategies to help make your listings pop, and I will cover those here.

The first is a powerful SEO strategy. When you write your listing description, every word you type will be entered into the MLS and syndicated across thousands of websites (that all rank highly on Google). Most agents never even think that a buyer might be searching for a special feature that your listing happens to have.

For example, during our most recent home search, my husband and I wanted to find a property with a home office. Specifically, we were looking for a room away from the home to provide space between our living and working areas. Thankfully, we just happened to stumble upon a house that checked this huge box on our wish list. Then we discovered a second home with an identical floor plan, just a few blocks away, in the same community. We loved both properties and wavered back and forth, trying to decide which one to buy. Ultimately we decided on the second. Ironically, once we moved in, we discovered that the home we purchased had everything else on our wish list: a drip irrigation system, water softener, reverse osmosis system, saltwater pool, hot water booster, craft room, and smart-home hard wiring—but the listing agent never mentioned any of these features in the MLS! If she had just taken the time to check a few boxes and write these features into the listing description, we would have found the second house sooner, and would have purchased it faster.

Moral of the story? If you want to drive more traffic to your listings, always include an accurate listing description that's SEO friendly.

Next, advertising should always be part of your marketing strategy whenever you acquire a new listing. Two ads work well to market your current listing (and help you acquire new ones). The first is the "Open House Ad," and the second is the "Just Listed Ad," which should be seen by everyone in the community. These ads will attract buyers to get the home sold quickly, but they'll also attract homeowners who are thinking about selling—so you can't go wrong.

MILESTONE #3: NEGOTIATION

Negotiation is the third step in the seller's journey. I can't say this enough: every seller wants more money in less time. To do that, be sure to negotiate the best terms and financially qualify every home buyer.

First, when you negotiate the best terms, you're ensuring that your seller is walking away with more money and less hassle. To do this, you must know the contract, inside and out. And again, if you're new, finding a mentor is a valuable investment in your education.

Second, before your seller accepts an offer, do your homework. Make sure that the buyer is highly qualified. I've entered escrow with an unqualified buyer and it was a nightmare. The buyer's bank declared bankruptcy in the middle of the transaction, which meant that we had to start all over with a second family, and pay two mortgages for a lot longer than we anticipated. It was an awful experience and it showed me what it could be like for a seller in the same position. Always do whatever you can to confirm qualifications and be honest with your sellers about any complications you may foresee.

HOW TO STAY ORGANIZED DURING NEGOTIATIONS

- Update your sellers daily.
- Confirm receipt of every offer.
- Save all offers in a shared folder.
- Ask buyers' agents qualifying questions.
- Present all offers in a timely manner.
- Walk through the offer with your sellers.
- Reach out to lenders.
- Ensure that the buyer has proof of funds.

If you can negotiate the best terms and be up front about buyer qualifications, you'll create a memorable client experience that a seller will rave about forever.

MILESTONE #4: TRANSACTION

The transaction is the fourth step in the seller's journey. Sellers want to be up to date on everything during escrow. Again, you do this every day, but a seller may only do this a handful of times in their entire life. And remember, if your clients don't know what's happening, they'll always assume the worst, so be sure to keep everyone in the loop. Again, several software tools on the market can automate this entire process for you.

To further eliminate the potential for fear and uncertainty, be available for all questions, inspections, and appraisals. Honesty and accountability are your two essential virtues when delivering an outstanding client experience. There are no perfect real estate transactions. When transactions go awry, be honest. When you or someone on your team drops the ball, take accountability. I can't stress this enough.

As long as you're honest and accountable with your sellers, they'll understand when things don't work out—even if they are upset. If they find out later, it will ruin the entire experience you have been working so hard to create.

MILESTONE #5: COMPENSATION

Compensation is the fifth step in the seller's journey. It goes without saying that sellers want to get paid on closing day. To ensure that this happens, monitor the progress of escrow very closely.

As an agent, I represented a family purchasing a new home, but they were dependent on another family to buy their current home, and the chain went on and on—adding up to four different families in this chain. Unfortunately, the first family in the chain had a little trouble with their lender on closing day, and every other family down the line had instant nightmares about being homeless. And, of course, the listing agent was nowhere to be found. Thankfully, the financing came through, but it was down to the wire, and everyone was shaking in their boots.

Every seller's worst nightmare is to miss closing—especially if they're contingent with multiple families in the contingency chain. Be available to your clients on closing day and be there to provide options if the transaction happens to go awry. You could do everything else right, but you'll break trust with the client if you're MIA on closing day.

MILESTONE #6: EVALUATION

Evaluation is the sixth step in the seller's journey. Remember, negative feedback is an opportunity to remove friction, and positive feedback shows you where to apply more force. Both activities allow you to accelerate your flywheel and gain more momentum in your business. Therefore, you should always be collecting client feedback consistently to improve your processes, procedures, programs, and people.

MILESTONE #7: COMMUNICATION

Communication is the seventh step in the seller's journey. It's crucial to stay in touch with past clients. This milestone solidifies it as part of the seller's journey and prepares your clients for these future contacts. So, again, reach out to all of your past clients once a quarter. We've found that this is the magic formula to keep you top of mind and allow you to generate more referrals.

FULL CIRCLE

In the past, agents relied heavily on the listing presentation to create an experience for sellers. But the seller experience needs to be designed much more holistically. Instead of putting on a show, try putting yourself in the client's shoes. First, think about how you want to be treated, then do that. That's how to create an amazing client experience!

FORCE VERSUS FRICTION

Apply Force: What levers create momentum in your business?

- Educating your sellers, so they know what to expect
- Having a rock-solid marketing strategy for every listing
- Pricing your listings strategically
- Presenting your listings beautifully online
- Optimizing your listing descriptions
- Negotiating the best terms
- Qualifying home buyers for every listing
- Keeping sellers up to date and in the loop during escrow
- Being available
- Being honest
- Being accountable
- Requesting feedback from sellers so you can improve
- Following up with past sellers once a quarter to stay top of mind

Avoid Friction: What levers slow momentum in your business?

- Not knowing your market
- Not communicating your value (before and after the listing appointment)
- Marketing listings without a plan
- Pricing listings without a strategy
- Not using professional photography
- Writing listing descriptions that are incomplete or unoptimized
- Failing to negotiate the best terms
- Having unorganized systems and processes
- Keeping sellers in the dark
- Not keeping sellers up to date and in the loop during escrow
- Being unavailable

- Being dishonest
- Being unaccountable
- Not requesting feedback from sellers so you can improve
- Failing to follow up with past sellers once a quarter to stay top of mind

STEP 6

TURN FANS INTO REFERRALS

6.1

THE ENDORSE STAGE

In the Endorse Stage, your clients not only embrace your brand, they proudly support it. These endorsements come in many forms, but the most common are word-of-mouth referrals, online reviews, testimonials, and shout-outs from other local businesses.

Raving fans are the most effective sales force for your business. They're like little referral engines that market your business for free! And the best part? When they send you new business, their referrals already know, like, trust, and remember you!

In the Endorse Stage, your single mission is to amplify your reach by making it easy for people to share experiences with your brand and rewarding them whenever they do.

That's typically done by deploying the following marketing tactics: (1) referrals, (2) online reviews, and (3) testimonials. In these final chapters, I'll show you how!

FULL CIRCLE

According to Qualtrics, 91 percent of people trust online reviews as much as they trust personal recommendations from friends.[7] The internet has forever changed the way word-of-mouth marketing works. Today, "word-of-mouth" means everything from online reviews to social media shout-outs. No matter where the referrals come from, getting them is vital if you want to reach 7-figures and beyond!

---

7 Diana Kaemingk, "Online Reviews Statistics to Know in 2022," Qualtrics, October 30, 2020, https://www.qualtrics.com/blog/online-review-stats.

FORCE VERSUS FRICTION

Apply Force: What levers create momentum in your business?

- Getting word-of-mouth referrals
- Getting online reviews
- Promoting testimonials
- Getting endorsements from local businesses

Avoid Friction: What levers slow momentum in your business?

- Creating a negative client experience
- Getting negative online reviews
- Not acquiring or promoting testimonials
- Not building relationships with other local businesses

6.2

AMPLIFY YOUR REFERRALS

A word-of-mouth referral comes from people who are so impressed with your brand that they feel compelled to tell others about it. Referrals are the best source of leads for your business because the conversion rate is high, and the cost per acquisition is low. And because multiple referrals can come from just one client, referrals are also a great accelerator that can fuel the exponential growth of your business.

There are so many different ways to get referrals these days; let's take a deeper look at them all.

REFERRAL SOURCES

- Repeat Business
- Client Referrals
- Agent Referrals
- Spousal Referrals
- Lender Referrals
- Local Business Referrals
- Lawyer Referrals
- Corporation Referrals
- Builder Referrals
- Landlord Referrals
- Military Referrals
- Government Referrals

REPEAT BUSINESS REFERRALS

Most agents don't think of repeat business as a referral, but it's actually one of the most powerful referrals you have, because the clients are referring *themselves*! Repeat business is amazing because the client already knows, likes, trusts, and remembers you. You also don't have to spend any significant amount of time, money, or effort to generate these sales because they come to you. Repeat clients can buy or sell multiple homes as part of the same transaction, or they can buy or sell multiple homes as part of a different transaction in the future.

The key to repeat business is that you have to stay top of mind to continue the relationship. Once the client forgets your name, you can forget getting their business again. So be sure to treat repeat clients well and reach out consistently—again, we recommend communication once a quarter.

CLIENT REFERRALS

Client referrals occur when a happy client suggests you to someone else. Client referrals are great because the leads are typically ready to move quickly. Think about it: once someone decides to make a move, the first thing they do is tell a friend. If they happen to be friends with one of your past clients, the hope is that your client will tell their friend about their amazing experience with you. The incredible client experience you've already provided to your existing and past clients should get you more referrals to their friends and family. And now you know how!

AGENT REFERRALS

Agent referrals come from out-of-town agents. When an agent doesn't service your area, they'll send you the lead, and you'll send them a finder's fee if the lead buys or sells a home. The benefit of an agent referral is that the lead is typically ready to make a move (and if they become happy clients, they may refer others).

The drawback with agent referrals is that the cost per acquisition is high—typically 20 percent to 30 percent. If you were to put that same amount of money into an online ad, you could probably get three to five new clients instead. But, of course, if a referral falls in your lap, you're not going to turn it away. In my experience, the two best sources of agent referrals are big conferences and online forums.

At conferences, we meet tons of wonderful agents from all over the world—the key is to follow up with all of them. Take the time to write them a handwritten card and be sure to mention a topic from the conversation you had with them, so they recall who you are.

Online forums are another referral source. When I was a working agent, I had a colleague that generated almost half of her business from real estate agent Facebook Groups. Every time someone posted a referral, she would be the first to respond. If you don't know which Facebook Groups to join, start with mine!

SPOUSAL REFERRALS

These referrals come from your partner or spouse. For example, one of my friends is an agent, and her husband works for a massive healthcare network. And when she first started, almost all of her business came exclusively from her husband's professional network. If your spouse works at a large company or happens to have an extensive sphere of influence, tap into that as a rich referral source.

LENDER REFERRALS

Banks are also in the real estate business because they sell home loans every day of the week. Many buyers start with finding a good lender, and then once they're qualified, they will need a good agent. If you create relationships with local lenders, you can be their go-to agent of choice. They can refer business to you—and you can refer business to them! Win-win.

LOCAL BUSINESS REFERRALS

Again, our members consistently highlight, promote, and support local businesses in their communities. And because our members are master marketers, they tend to drive tons of traffic to these local businesses. As a result, the business owners feel compelled to return the favor. They promote our members on their platforms, sending tons of leads, clients, and referrals in return. When you grow a massive following, local businesses will want to work with you too. And if you get in the habit of giving, it always comes back!

LAWYER REFERRALS

Lawyers are another source of referrals. When unfortunate events occur, like a death or divorce, people are often burdened by an accompanying home sale. To help their clients through the process, lawyers will often refer their clients to agents they know and trust.

In my last brokerage, an agent worked in a broad geographic area because she had an extremely narrow niche: helping irate spouses during messy divorces. She even has a local radio show, popular blog, and YouTube channel dedicated to it. Her branding is so strong that every divorce lawyer in the region knows to send their clients to her. Over the years, she's developed symbiotic relationships with these lawyers and has remained the top agent in that brokerage for years.

If you develop strong relationships with these lawyers and stay top of mind, they can be an infinite source of referrals for your business too!

CORPORATION/GOVERNMENT REFERRALS

Large corporations have employees relocating between offices constantly. Many of them will work with agents as relocation specialists. When employees move into the area, these agents will help them buy a home, and when employees move away from the area, they'll help employees sell. Government and military referrals work similarly.

In the '80s, my parents worked with an agent who specialized in helping professional athletes in Los Angeles. Whenever the team recruited a new player (or transferred one away), every athlete on the team knew who to call. This agent developed strong relationships with every client, and referrals from their team kept coming.

Government niches work similarly. As government employees move in and out of town and military service members move on and off base, relocation agents are on standby to help.

These referral sources are challenging to acquire initially because these organizations typically only work with a handful of agents at a time. But if you can get your foot in the door with either the organization or its employees, you'll have referral business for life.

BUILDER REFERRALS

Home builders are a great source of referrals too. First, most buyers who walk into a newly built home walk away without buying. But the home builder isn't interested in working any of those buyer leads. That equates to tens or even hundreds of hot leads that are literally thrown away. If you work with a sales rep who can hand these leads to you, you've got an ongoing referral source.

Second, sometimes buyers will buy the newly built home, but they need to sell their current home to make the move. But builders aren't interested in working any of those leads either. That's a ton of seller leads that end up in the trash every year. But again, if you can work with a sales rep to hand these leads over to you, you've got a great referral source.

LANDLORD REFERRALS

Landlords and property managers are in the business of real estate as well. Every day, they encounter hardworking tenants saving up to buy a home. When you build strong relationships with these landlords and tenants, you have an instant referral source you can tap into. I also know agents who work rentals exclusively—the commissions aren't great, but when the tenant is ready to buy, it really pays off.

FULL CIRCLE

As you can probably tell, referrals can come from just about anywhere. And the best news is that there's no trick to getting these referrals.

The best way to encourage referrals is simply to stay top of mind. If no one remembers you, no one will refer anyone to you. Be sure to show gratitude for all the referral attempts you receive and acknowledge all the referrals you close. You can send a gift card in different amounts for both. For your best referrers, you can reward them with something special, like an invitation to an exclusive event. No matter what you decide, be sure to express gratitude in a meaningful way. These are your VIPs, and they deserve to feel special. Finally, before you start gifting, read up on your local laws and regulations to stay in compliance.

In essence, the formula for getting referrals is simple:

1. Show up for your clients.
2. Be visible in your community.
3. Create an amazing experience.
4. Respond with gratitude for the referrals that come your way.

FORCE VERSUS FRICTION

Apply Force: What levers create momentum in your business?

- Building strong relationships with referral partners
- Staying top of mind with referral partners
- Expressing gratitude for referrals

Avoid Friction: What levers slow momentum in your business?

- Abandoning relationships with referral partners
- Failing to stay top of mind with referral partners
- Not expressing gratitude for referrals

6.3

AMPLIFY YOUR ONLINE REVIEWS

For the first time in history, strangers have as much influence as friends. And past clients have massive influence over future clients—even though they've never met. Let that sink in.

Strangers now influence our behavior, making online reviews a new type of referral that can make or break your business. One negative review can repel your revenue for the foreseeable future. Clients now have a platform to explain their pain and frustrations, democratizing information through online reviews.

Online reviews are holding all agents accountable. This is why it's so important to act in extreme integrity and put your clients first. The client should be at the center of your flywheel and every decision you make should enhance the client's experience.

You should work toward removing friction daily. If you fail to identify pain points in your business privately, past clients will share them publicly. Online reviews are now a permanent part of our culture. When done right, they have the potential to provide powerful social proof that will amplify your reach and create massive momentum in your business.

Positive reviews are the best insurance policy. They're the best way to brace your business against (inevitable) negative reviews in the future. Some clients are impossible to please and won't stop until the world becomes aware. So it's crucial to acquire tons of positive reviews now, to dilute negative reviews later.

For example, if you have no reviews now and get a 1-star review tomorrow, every search on the internet will expose your 1-star brand. However, if you have twenty 5-star reviews now and get a 1-star review tomorrow, you'll still have a 4.8-star brand. The second scenario is easy to bounce back from, but the first would be a debilitating blow. To insure against this, acquire as many 5-star reviews as you can now as an insurance policy for the future.

Most agents have incomplete profiles on all of these review sites because they think that the benefits don't outweigh the drawbacks. I get it. It's a considerable risk to promote your brand on these platforms and risk getting negative exposure. But after working with tens of thousands of agents over the years, I can confidently tell you that ignoring these sites is a mistake. You'll begin to rank on these review sites if you optimize your business listing. And once you start showing up in searches, these sites can be an incredible source of leads, clients, and referrals. I've worked with agents who get almost half of their business from their FREE Yelp profile! So ranking on these sites is definitely worth it.

These review sites also rank well in search engines. Meaning, if you rank well on a review site, and that site ranks well on Google, your brand is just two clicks away from the front page of Google. Don't forget that voice assistants, like Siri and Alexa, rely on these sites to pull information too.

Did you know that anyone in the world can add your business to these review sites? They can add all your information (and a review) without your permission. This means that people can review you whether you decide to participate or not. Zillow, Facebook, Google, and Yelp may already have you listed in their directories! So you might as well lean in before the negative reviews come.

This brings me to my last point: when you have an unclaimed business profile, many of these sites use it as a billboard to advertise your competitors. Yes, when people find your listing, your competitors might be showing up on your profile. So claiming your business and completing your profiles will allow you to take more control of your online reputation positively.

HOW TO GET MORE ONLINE REVIEWS

Most agents want all of their clients to review them on one site—like Zillow. But every review site runs on algorithms. If your client hasn't been previously active on Zillow, their review may get buried, so it's always best to give clients a choice. Have clients review you on sites where they are most active. If you let the client choose, there's a greater chance that the review will get posted and seen.

ONLINE REVIEW PLATFORMS:

Yelp

Facebook

Google My Business

Zillow

Realtor.com

WHEN TO ASK FOR ONLINE REVIEWS

Tell your clients from the very beginning that you'll be working hard to create an incredible client experience that earns a glowing review. As soon as the transaction closes, your clients will immediately move toward the Evaluation Milestone in their customer journey. This is the perfect time to ask for the review.

Shoot them a link to your digital evaluation form, and technology takes care of the rest. If the client responds positively, add a logic jump to the form that redirects them to their favorite review site. If the client responds negatively, add a logic jump that redirects them to a thank-you page instead. This way, you can promote positive feedback in public (and negative feedback in private).

If you don't get the review immediately after asking, gently remind them throughout the Communication Milestone until you do. To make it even easier, offer to draft the review on their behalf—but be sure to let them post it on their own.

HANDLING NEGATIVE REVIEWS

At this point, you've learned tons of processes to avoid negative reviews, but if you stay in business long enough, they're bound to happen. The key is to handle them with kindness and grace. Always respond politely to negative reviews to show that you care about the client's experience. Always respond calmly with the intent to resolve the problem. Ask to resolve the issue via private message, text, or phone call. Once the problem has been resolved, and your client feels better about their experience, gently ask them to update their review.

Remember, the best insurance policy for a negative review is lots of positive reviews that have already been posted. Start building up your reviews today to insure against negative reviews tomorrow.

PROMOTING POSITIVE REVIEWS

An outstanding online reputation is powerful social proof. Use these positive reviews as a strategic tool in your marketing arsenal by promoting them anywhere that future clients can see them.

PLACES TO PROMOTE POSITIVE REVIEWS

Your website

Your print marketing materials

Ads

Social media

Everywhere else you can think of!

FULL CIRCLE

A couple of years ago, my husband and I were in Nashville, Tennessee, at a big marketing conference. When the event

paused for lunch, we raced out of the conference room because we were starving. Not knowing where we were (or what we were doing), we started walking aimlessly, looking for food. We stumbled upon this little sandwich shop and decided to step in to grab lunch. As soon as we walked through the door, I got a weird vibe (along with a strange smell) and immediately went into full retreat—with my husband in tow. After our whirlwind exit, he looked at me and said, "Let me find something on Yelp." He found an excellent spot with tons of great reviews, and it was literally the best BBQ I'd ever tasted.

It got me thinking, though: we're so dependent on reviews as a society. We check them first—like second nature. If I couldn't even buy a sandwich without first checking reviews, there's no way I would ever hire an agent without checking reviews either. I'm sure your future clients feel the same.

FORCE VERSUS FRICTION

Apply Force: What levers create momentum in your business?

- Creating an amazing client experience
- Claiming and completing your business profiles
- Getting positive reviews early and often
- Handling negative reviews gracefully
- Promoting positive reviews strategically in your marketing plan

Avoid Friction: What levers slow momentum in your business?

- Failing to put clients first
- Ignoring or neglecting your profile on review sites

- Waiting until you get a negative review to take action
- Handling negative reviews gracelessly
- Not utilizing positive reviews in your marketing strategy

6.4

AMPLIFY YOUR TESTIMONIALS

Testimonials can be a powerful referral tool in your marketing toolbox. A testimonial is a glowing recommendation from a past client, and it's the next best thing to a word-of-mouth referral.

A testimonial is different from an online review because it's a piece of content you own, which means it can be shared and promoted. There are so many other benefits of having testimonials. Let's talk about each of them below.

First, when clients take the time to give you a testimonial, it strengthens the relationship they have with your brand. When you capture their sentiments on camera, it becomes a memorable shared experience between you and the client.

Second, since testimonials are in the client's own words, they appear less like a sales pitch and more like a natural referral. Don't overlook the fact that a referral from a stranger has just as much influence as a referral from a friend.

Third, testimonials can be promoted, shared, and marketed effortlessly online across all your branded platforms. We have members using their testimonials as ads, social media marketing, and even SEO. Testimonials posted on your website and review sites can get ranked easily and seen by many.

Finally, when you give clients a framework to rave about your brand, it becomes much easier for them to recall that framework when they refer you. Give them a few talking points, then have them film or write their testimonial. Remember, your brand is the essence of what people say when you're not in the room. So if you give them a viable framework, they'll know exactly what to say.

FULL CIRCLE

People trust reviews from real people. According to BigCommerce, 72 percent of consumers say positive testimonials and reviews increase their trust in a business[8]—that's huge. Showing your community evidence of the positive experiences your clients have had with you instills trust in your brand. That means they're more likely to turn to you for their real estate needs. But you'll never get testimonials unless you ask. And those testimonials won't do you any good unless you share them. So, request, capture, and promote the testimonials you get from your happy clients.

---

8 Emily Cullinan, "How to Use Customer Testimonials to Generate 62% More Revenue From Every Customer, Every Visit," BigCommerce, accessed November 22, 2021, https://www.bigcommerce.com/blog/customer-testimonials.

FORCE VERSUS FRICTION

Apply Force: What levers create momentum in your business?

- Requesting, capturing, and promoting client testimonials

Avoid Friction: What levers slow momentum in your business?

- Not leveraging testimonials as a powerful marketing tool in your business

STEP 7

GAIN INFINITE MOMENTUM

We call ourselves Community Influencer® because we believe that real estate agents have the power to influence their communities. Our members are the anchors in their communities, and they're making an impact every day.

They lead with relationships instead of real estate, trust instead of transactions, and compassion instead of contracts.

They connect with people every day and serve them by providing value. And because they give before they receive, that value comes back in the form of leads, clients, and referrals.

They don't have to sell themselves to leads because their leads are already sold. They don't have to chase clients because clients chase them.

They're highly visible and always top of mind.

Attention is the new currency. When you pay attention to your community, your community pays attention to you. And when you build that community, both online and off, all eyes are on you.

Everyone wants to work with influencers because influencers are magnets that attract attention.

We've seen members, just like you, get the attention of:

- Local shops, restaurants, and charities
- Prominent politicians
- TV networks
- Big brands
- Small brands
- Local magazines
- Major newspapers
- And more!

We've also seen members get:

- Paid sponsorships
- Brand deals
- Cast on popular TV shows
- Featured in magazines, podcasts, and radio shows

They've even won prestigious awards.

When you prioritize community, the community responds. When you serve, you'll grow your following exponentially.

As you build an audience, you'll gain notoriety in your community. And this notoriety will allow you to scale your business infinitely.

I want you to command so much influence that everyone will want to work with you! Not just buyers and sellers. Everyone.

Your influencer status will allow you to:

- Attract people to your brand in droves
- Create leads on demand
- And ultimately take over any local market you set your sights on

If you think of any top producer or celebrity agent, they all have one thing in common. They've all mastered their marketing. Some of these agents have even gone on to build empires.

You can do the same.

Through the lens of a simple flywheel framework, you now have a real estate marketing model that will allow you to attract an infinite number of leads, clients, and referrals to scale your real estate business to 7-figures and beyond. And you can do it all by simply being yourself, having more fun, and making a difference.

You've now learned how to:

- Build a magnetic brand
- Attract leads to your list
- Convert those leads into clients
- Transform clients into fans
- And turn fans into referrals

Now that you have all the tools you need to accelerate your business, go out and create momentum!

If you want my help, you can find me here:
CommunityInfluencer.com

Until then, think big!

Made in United States
North Haven, CT
28 November 2023